Clicking with Your Dog

Step-by-Step in Pictures

Clicking with Your Dog

Step-by-Step in Pictures

Written and
illustrated by

Peggy Tillman

Dedicated to Prince (1956-1971)
the dog who taught me

Clicking with Your Dog

Library of Congress Cataloging-in-Publication Data is available.
Library of Congress Card Number: 00-108594

ISBN 1-890948-08-X

Sunshine Books, Inc.
49 River Street, Suite #3
Waltham, MA 02453
www.clickertraining.com

20 19 18 17 16 15 14 13 12 11

Contents

Chapter 4   **Other Practical Skills**   67

Teach these additional skills to keep you and your dog happy
and healthy.

Table and Chart List

Introduction

As editor and publisher of this book I am proud to be able to introduce Peggy Tillman, author, illustrator, and clicker training teacher, to dog lovers everywhere.

Peggy has put almost 100 behaviors in this book. These are not competitive skills, but the things every dog needs to know, and a lot more that are just plain fun. Some behaviors are shown in three versions: for example, three different clicker-based ways to get a dog to walk on a loose leash. The most common behavior problems are charted and cross-indexed so you can see at a glance several possible positive approaches to what you want to get rid of.

Peggy's drawings are as simple and charming as her writing. If you generally prefer to skip written instructions, a glance at the marginal notes will show you what each behavior is good for. Then you can see how to clicker train it, including the all-important timing of the click, just by looking at the pictures.

There is also a lot of common sense in this book. The Dog's Bill of Rights explains things that many new pet owners are unaware of. A dog needs its own place to sleep. Dogs get tired and need privacy. Dogs can get bored and lonely. The owner should meet those needs, and clicker games are an easy and natural way to do so.

This book is a great answer to any perplexed pet owner who is willing to give the clicker a try. You might just use five or six of the ideas in the book, and still transform your relationship with the dog. As Peggy puts it, "If you've got that clicker in your hand, you are automatically looking for something good to click. That alone is going to change your relationship. And when the dog GETS it, all of a sudden it's the smartest dog in the world."

You will find that you truly understand your dog at last; and thanks to the clicker, the dog will understand you, too. A bridge has been built, and it will last a lifetime.

Karen Pryor

Chapter 1
Find a Better Way

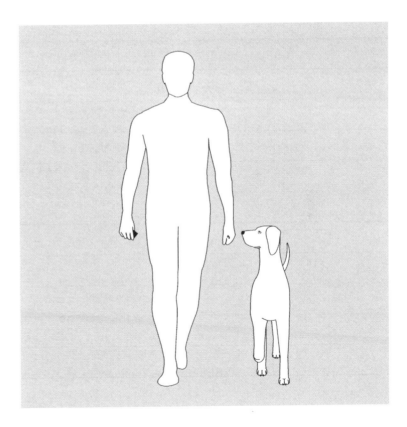

Training with Games, the Clicker Way

Learning is finding out what you already know

— Richard Bach

Have you noticed how quickly your dog figured out that the door bell means someone is coming into the house? Or what the can opener means? Or what is going to happen when you put on a coat or when you take out a suitcase? It seems almost magical when they learn these things so fast. Dogs are intelligent animals. This book is going to show you how to use that dog intelligence to your advantage.

To create this learning magic we use a small plastic clicker that makes a unique sound when you press it (see clicker supplies on page 194 for information on obtaining clickers). The clicker is a marker signal. It tells your dog "Yes, that is what I want you to do," and promises him a reward for doing it. It is like the camera click that captures the exact action you want.

Clicker training is a simple proven way to communicate with your dog using positive reinforcement. Clicker training is based on scientific research in the laws of learning and ***operant conditioning*** (see page 185).

In 1985, dolphin trainer Karen Pryor wrote a book, *Don't Shoot the Dog*, about applied operant conditioning (see page 194). She explained how anyone using this learning theory could train a variety of animals, including people, without force. This book changed how people looked at dog training. By 1992 dog trainers began using clicker training that they learned at seminars given by Karen Pryor.

While the clicker is new to dog training, the clicker (or some event marker) has been used in training marine animals and birds for years. Most of the animal actors on TV and in the movies are now clicker trained. Many service animals that help the disabled, and many working dogs such as police dogs, are also clicker trained.

You don't have to understand the scientific theory to apply clicker training. Young children sometimes make excellent clicker trainers. However, if you are interested in understanding more about operant conditioning, there are many clearly written explanations of applied operant conditioning (see Books, page 193.)

Now for the fun part: Teaching the games. To the dog, clicker training is all one big wonderful game. The game is simple: You have something your dog wants, and he must do something for you, to get it.

The games in this book have specific instructions. However, every person and dog is different. No one way will work for all. Find the method that works best for you and your dog. If none of them work, be creative. Experiment until you find a way to get your dog doing what you want. Don't use force. If you use punishment, your dog will not want to play the game. Remember what Grandmother said: "You catch more flies with honey than with vinegar."

With clicker training we name the action after your dog has learned what to do. This is unlike traditional training in which we give a command before the dog learns the skill. In clicker training we wait until we are sure the dog understands what he is supposed to do. Then we teach him a 'cue'. The cue can be either a **hand signal** or a **verbal cue** (see page 182 for more information on cues).

People often ask "Do I have to carry around a clicker all the time?" I asked this myself when I first learned about clicker training. The answer is no. The clicker is a teaching tool. When your dog understands what you want, you no longer need to use the clicker for that skill. However, I am still carrying around clickers because it is so much fun to teach new things to my canine friends.

Ann, Andy, and Arf will help you learn to play the games. Let the games begin!

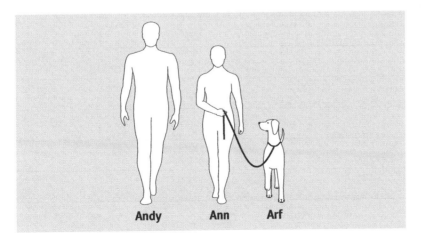

Andy   **Ann**   **Arf**

How to Use This Book

Just Do It

— Nike Ad

Some of us are very impatient (like me) and just want to get started. We're only interested in solving one or two problems. We don't want to learn everything there is to know about a subject. We just want to write a simple letter with our new computer program. We don't care how it works or about all the possibilities it offers. Others however, want all the information they can get before starting a project. They want to know everything there is about the computer program. I've designed this book so both types can find the information they need.

Think of this book as being like a cookbook. Browse the book or go straight to the instructions that you need the most right now. Be sure to look up the words in bold italics in the Tips and Terms section (page 179). These pages give detailed information, such as how to add cues.

Here are five recommended options for using this book. Pick the option that meets your needs.

1. Help! I have a problem with my dog. I need help RIGHT NOW!	• Read Fast Start (pages 8–19) to learn what you need. • Find what you want to change on the Solutions Chart (page 17). • Select a game or skill you want to teach and begin clicking.
2. I haven't trained a dog before and I want to get started right away.	• Read Fast Start (pages 8–19) to learn what you need. • Begin with Capture Something Cute (page 94). Learn how to communicate with your dog while having fun. • When you are both ready, show off to your friends.
3. I have an extremely active dog. I can't wear him out.	• Read Fast Start (pages 8–19) to learn what you need. • Teach several Useful Tricks (page 91). Clicker training is mental exercise and often helps with overactive dogs. • Read Exercise (page 168) and Jobs (page 166).
4. I want to get started right away, however I want to learn more about clicker training before starting.	• Skim the entire book. • Select a couple of tricks and teach them to your dog. • After training a couple of tricks, read Super Clicking (page 119). • See Resources for more information on clicker training (page 191).
5. I want to learn everything I can about clicker training.	• Skim the book • Teach your dog a trick or two (page 91–117). • Teach your dog anything else he needs to know from the book. • Read the Super Clicking chapter (page 119–137). • Read the Tips and Terms chapter (page 178–189). • Use the books and videos in Resources (page 193–194). • Use the Internet to learn more about clicker training (page 192). • Join an e-mail list (page 191). • Show off your wonderful clicker trained canine friend.

Chapter 2
Fast Start

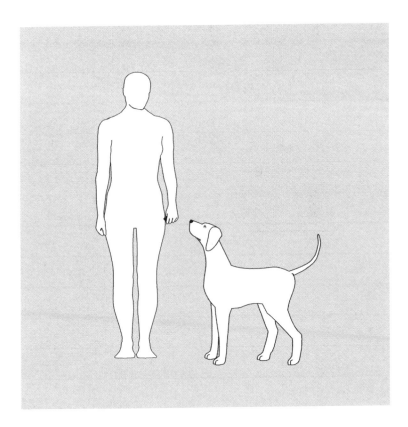

What You Will Need

You will need three things to get started. You need a dog, a clicker, and treats.

Dog

Dogs are never too old or too young to learn clicker training. Puppies have been clicker trained from birth, although starting puppies when their ears and eyes are open is best. Some breeders are sending eight-week-old clicker trained puppies to their new homes. These puppies know sit and down, and are house trained. Old dogs find clicker games very stimulating and exciting. Even dogs with disabilities can learn. Trainers often use a flashlight instead of a clicker to teach deaf dogs.

Clicker

Clickers are inexpensive plastic devices that sound like a child's toy. They are simple to use. Even very young children can use clickers. Be careful, kids love them and clickers have been known to disappear into children's rooms, pockets, and backpacks.

To use the clicker, simply press on the flat end of metal tongue. Don't hold the tongue down. Click only once. Don't do multiple clicks.

You can purchase clickers from several sources. The Resources section of this book lists places to order them. Many clicker web sites can help you find them. Be sure to purchase more than one clicker. Having extra clickers is handy.

Treats

See the list for Treats on page 11.

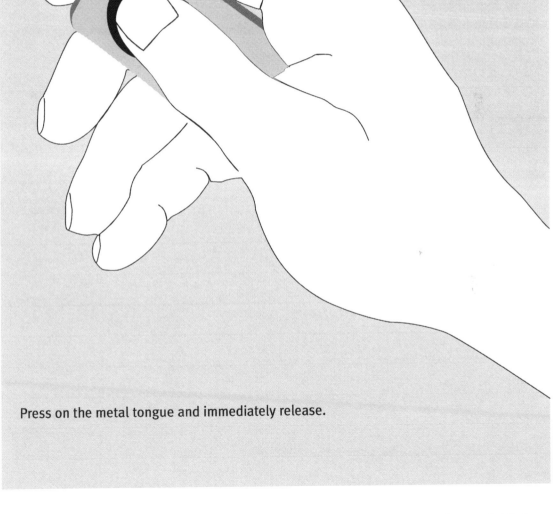

Press on the metal tongue and immediately release.

Treats

Police officer and dog trainer Steve White suggested some of these treats. Some suggestions came from other clicker trainers and some are treats that I use. I suggest you take your dog on a tour of the kitchen and see what he likes. You can use almost any food (no chocolate). The food treat should be no larger than a raisin. Toys can be used, but they can slow training. Vary treats often. In very distracting environments use the treats your dog likes best. Be sure to supervise him while he is playing with toys.

Foods

Cooked chicken pieces (boneless)

Pieces of homemade cookies or biscuits

Cheerios and other similar sized cereals

Pounce cat treats

Chopped carrots or green beans

Kibble dog food

Diced Chicken

Diced Hot Dog

String cheese

Leftover steak pieces

Hard-boiled eggs

Sardines

Commercial dog treats

Corn Nuts

Wheat Thins

Cheese Whiz

Popcorn

French fries

Ice cubes

Bread crust

Croutons

Rice cakes

Peanut butter

Canned cat food (use a spoon)

Broken fortune cookie pieces

Cooked pasta (many forms)

Rice balls

Canned chicken

Crumbled ground beef

Objects and toys

Tennis balls

Kongs (see page 163)

Rope tugs

Dried liver

Boat bumpers

Buoys

Bicycle tires

Burlap sacks

Puppy tugs

Leashes

Street-hockey balls

Hockey pucks

Soccer balls

Basketballs

Bully balls (see page 165)

Buster Cubes (see page 165)

Paper bags

Squeaker toys

Frisbees

Teaching the Click

It's okay to make mistakes. Mistakes are our teachers—they help us learn.

— John Bradshaw

The following are two ways to teach your dog the meaning of the clicker.

Method One

This method teaches your dog that the click means that he will get a treat. Begin by holding small treats in one hand (or on a table very close by). Click the clicker *once* and give a treat. From now on *never* click without giving a treat. This is extremely important. Your dog will soon learn that the click is a promise of a treat. Don't break your promise to him! Continue clicking and treating until you notice that he is looking at the clicker instead of the treat. He will look as if he is saying "Hurry up and click that thing so I can get my treat."

Method Two

This method teaches the meaning of the click and teaches a skill. Pick something from the book that you want your dog to do. It can be looking at you, sitting, or some cute thing he does. Click when your dog does what you want and then give him a treat. Continue clicking and giving treats every time your dog repeats the action you want.

If you make a mistake with either method, just laugh and try again. Remember this is a fun game to your dog. However, be sure that you click only for what you want him to repeat. If you click just as he begins to get up from a sit, you will be telling him that you will reward getting up. Be careful of what you click. You will get it!

One of the best ways I have heard to improve the timing of your clicks is to practice with a VCR. Freeze the action on a tape with the pause button on the remote control.

Note: Muffle the clicker if the sound startles your dog. You can muffle it by wrapping a towel around it, putting it in your pocket, or holding it behind your back.

click!

Click the clicker once

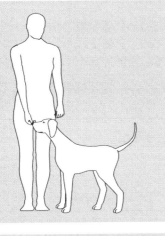

Give a treat

When your dog begins looking at the clicker before you click, he understands the clicker.

Sessions

Nothing is particularly hard if you divide it into it into small steps.

— Henry Ford

It is very important to keep teaching sessions short. Current learning theory studies show that learning is best done in short sessions. Dogs seem to do best with sessions only three to five minutes long. Longer sessions are not productive. Clicker training can be mentally exhausting for dogs. Young puppies have very short attention spans and may need even shorter session times.

If your dog loses interest and wanders off during the teaching session, be patient. Wait to see if he comes back on his own. It may be a *learning dip* (see page 184). A learning dip is a normal part of learning. Or, it could be because your dog is tired. If he doesn't come back in a few minutes, end the session. Try again later. If this happens often, consider using more exciting and motivating treats.

I understand that there are many demands for your time. Traditional dog training (mostly drill) can be very difficult to work into busy a schedule. However, because clicker training is done in several short sessions, working it into your daily schedule is easy.

See the table to the right for an example of how training can fit into your average workday. Whatever schedule you use, remember that play always creates an eagerness to learn.

Example Day	
6:00-6:05 A.M.	While taking your dog out for his bathroom break, practice coming when called by making it a game. Hide from him. Click and give him a treat when he finds you. Do this one to three times.
6:15-6:18 A.M.	Play a game while you are having breakfast. You could ask him to go to his mat, sit, or even do a fun trick. Click and treat.
6:30-6:35 A.M.	Ask him to lie down while you are getting dressed. If he is just learning, ask for several 10-second downs. As he gets better, ask him to stay in the down position until you are finished dressing. Don't forget to click and treat.
7:00-7:01 A.M.	Feed him his breakfast. Give him a challenge. Stuff his food in Kongs or have the kids hide it in the backyard. If you give him his food all at once, ask for a skill he knows before putting it down. It could be a trick or a sit-stay. Give him a release word or a click and let him eat (treat).

Work	
5:45-6:30 P.M.	Change your clothes and relax for a few minutes. Play retrieving games with him or take him for a walk or run. Ask him for sits, stays, gives, and anything else you are working on, while playing with him. Be sure to treat.
6:30-6:35 P.M.	During your dinner, click and treat for a new skill, such as going to his mat or crate.
7:00-7:01 P.M.	Feed your dog his dinner and repeat what you did for his breakfast.
8:00-10:30 P.M.	Play games with him. If you are watching television, you can use the commercials to train a game. **TOTAL SESSIONS: EIGHT**

Clicker Solutions Chart

My dog training students often ask how to change their dog's inappropriate actions. I always suggest they teach their dog a behavior they like, instead of trying to stop what they don't like.

Clicker trainers don't focus on stopping inappropriate conduct. We train a substitute action we like for ones we don't like. For example, a dog can't jump and sit at the same time. So we teach our dogs to sit when guests arrive.

To do this, decide what you want your dog to do. If your dog's barking is driving you crazy, your first reaction is to plead (or yell) to get him to be quiet. You are trying to stop conduct you don't want. To change your dog's behavior you must take a positive action instead of just reacting.

I have listed clicker solutions for the ten most common behavior problems. Be creative; if one game on the chart doesn't take you to your goal, choose another solution. All dogs and all teachers are different. Find the best way for you and your dog.

	Solutions		
Jumping on people	Polite Puppy, page 36	Go to Your Mat, page 34	Stay, page 54
Pulling on the leash	Make Like a Tree, page 38	Loose Leash Walking, page 40	Penalty Yards, page 42
House training	House Training, page 80	Bell Signal, page 82	Crate Training, page 78
Chewing	Chewing, page 140	Leave It, page 62	Crate Training, page 78

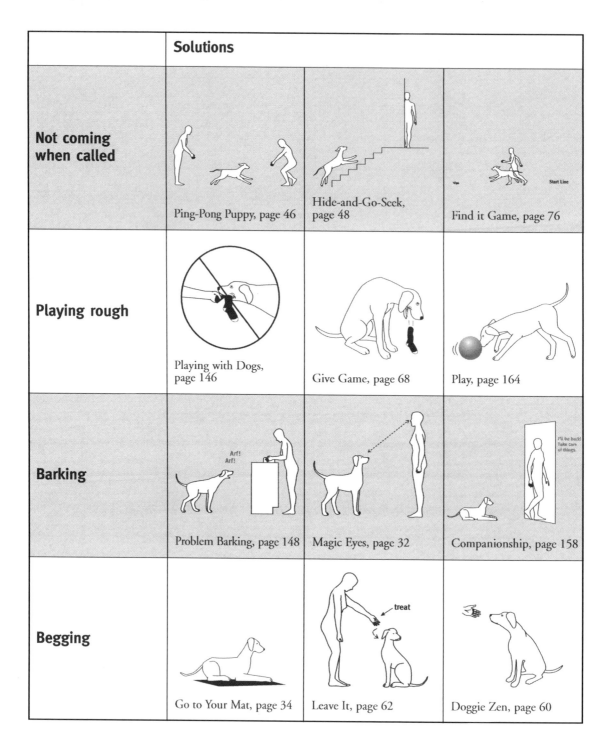

	Solutions		
Not coming when called	Ping-Pong Puppy, page 46	Hide-and-Go-Seek, page 48	Find it Game, page 76
Playing rough	Playing with Dogs, page 146	Give Game, page 68	Play, page 164
Barking	Problem Barking, page 148	Magic Eyes, page 32	Companionship, page 158
Begging	Go to Your Mat, page 34	Leave It, page 62	Doggie Zen, page 60

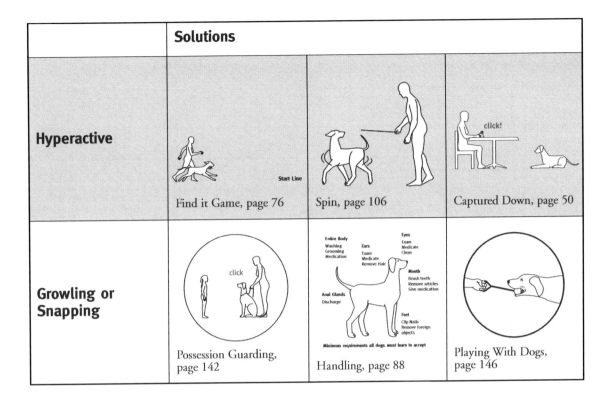

	Solutions		
Hyperactive	Find it Game, page 76	Spin, page 106	Captured Down, page 50
Growling or Snapping	Possession Guarding, page 142	Handling, page 88	Playing With Dogs, page 146

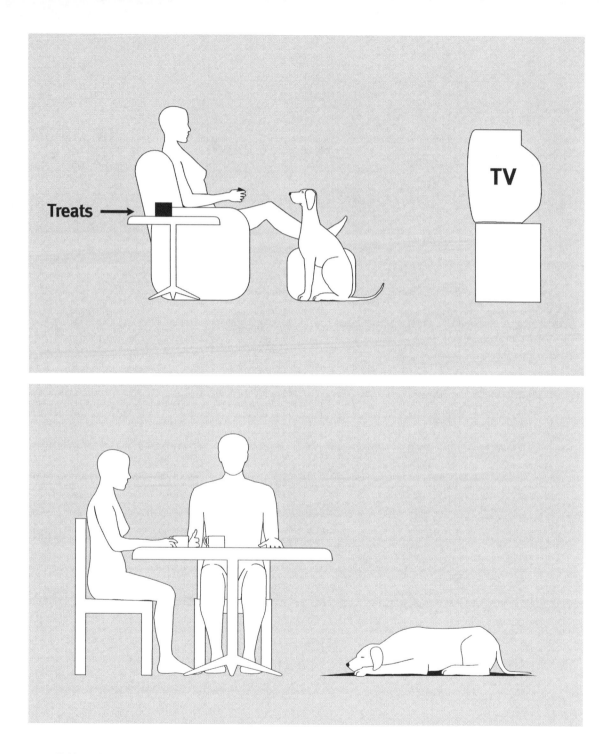

Treats ←

TV

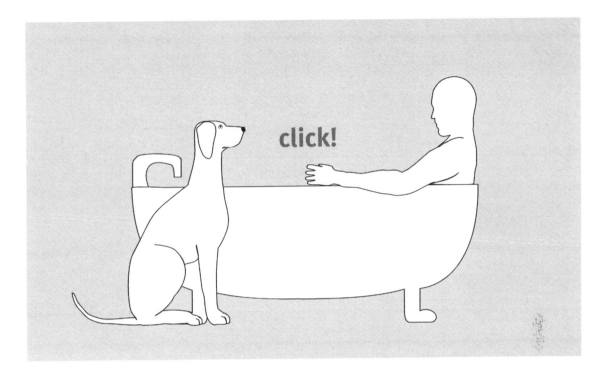

**There is always time
for clicker training!**

– Karen Pryor

Chapter 3
Manners

People Manners for Dogs

We all want polite dogs. We want them to behave well in public and at home. However, dog manners and people manners are different.

Most dogs know dog manners. They learn them from their mother and other dogs. However, people must teach dogs to understand people manners. For example, puppies learn that it is good dog manners to jump up and lick an adult dog's face. If we don't want our dogs to jump on us and lick our faces, we must show them how to act around people. The easiest way to do this is by teaching them games like Polite Puppy on page 36.

Eye contact is another example. In dog manners staring directly at another dog is not polite. Yet we want our dogs to look directly at us (see page 32).

Learning people manners is important for all dogs that live with humans. Clicker trainer Sue Ailsby explains the importance of teaching good manners this way: "Training does not limit a dog, training frees a dog. My dog is not limited because she does what I tell her. She is free: free to ride with me, free to walk with me, free to meet people, free to run off lead in the park, free to play with other dogs. The untrained dog is 'free' to sit in the backyard all by itself."

We teach dogs our manners with the same method that he learned his doggie manners: Positive consequences. It simply means your dog must figure out how to earn a reward. For example, if I want to teach "Go to your mat," I click and give him a reward for lying calmly on his mat. The reward could be a treat, a bone, or favorite toy. He will quickly figure out that "good things happen when I stay on this mat."

On the following pages you will find a variety of ways to show your canine companion basic people manners. Experiment with the different lessons to find the ones that work best for you and your dog. Be sure to have fun and reward both yourself and your dog for learning.

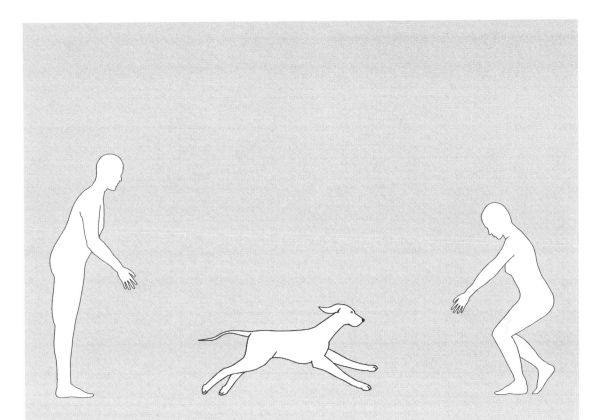

In order to really enjoy a dog, one doesn't merely try to train him to be semihuman. The point of it is to open oneself to the possibility of becoming partly a dog.

— Edward Hoagland (1932) American Novelist

Sit: Magnet Method

Uses

Stopping jumping

Teaching wait or stay

Grooming

Putting on leashes

Having the dog wait to be fed

To teach a sit using the magnet method, hold a small treat in one hand while facing your dog. With your dog in a standing position, hold your hand with the treat in it above his nose. Then slowly move your hand between his ears. Your dog will look up to see the treat. He will lower his hind legs into a sit. The instant his bottom hits the ground, click. Toss the treat to one side, so that he has to get up to get it.

After he sits several times in a row, make the same motion but without a treat in your hand. Click and treat when he sits.

When your dog is sitting every time you have the clicker or treats, it is time to begin telling him to sit. Clicker trainers call this a *cue* (page 182). When you use the magnet method, the easiest cue to teach is a **hand signal** (page 183). Your hand motion becomes the signal or cue to your dog to sit.

If you wish to teach a **verbal cue** (page 182) wait until your dog's rear starts down, but before it hits the floor, then say "Sit." After saying "Sit" several times as his bottom hits the floor, begin asking him to "Sit" before he starts sitting. Click and treat when he sits. If your dog sits and you have not given him the cue, don't click and treat. Click and treat only if he sits after you have given the cue.

Saying the cue loudly or repeatedly is not necessary. I have found a really effective and impressive way to teach the cue. Whisper it. A dog's hearing is far superior to ours so we don't have to shout. As Colonel Sherman T. Potter on the MASH television program once said, "Someone who doesn't understand English doesn't understand loud English either."

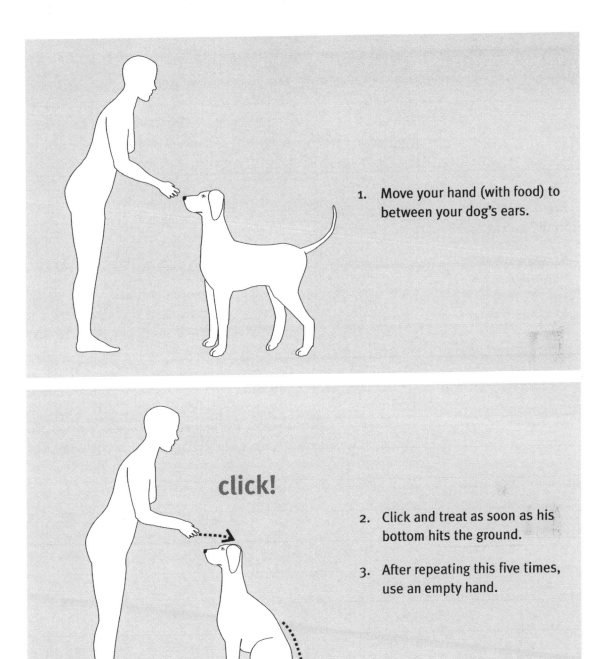

1. Move your hand (with food) to between your dog's ears.

click!

2. Click and treat as soon as his bottom hits the ground.

3. After repeating this five times, use an empty hand.

Sit: Capture Method

Uses

Preventing barking

Keeping your dog safe

Keeping your dog calm

This is the fun way to train. Clicker trainers call it the lazy trainer method or couch training. It is really easy. However, you need to observe your dog carefully.

To use this method you simply get a bowl of treats, your clicker, and a comfortable spot. I've even taught from the bathtub. Then settle down and wait until your dog sits. Don't give him any signal or say anything to him. When he sits, click the second his bottom hits the floor. Then toss him a treat so he must get up to get it. This allows you to repeat the whole procedure. The goal is to reward as many sits as possible in the shortest amount of time.

One of my favorite ways to begin teaching this is to watch TV with a bowl of popcorn. During the commercials you click and treat your dog for sitting. Commercials are about three minutes, so it is perfect timing for your session. The next session, try another location so your dog doesn't think you expect him to sit only when you are watching TV.

When your dog is sitting for you every time you pick up the clicker or have treats, begin adding a *signal* or *verbal cue*. The instructions for how to add the cues can be found on page 182.

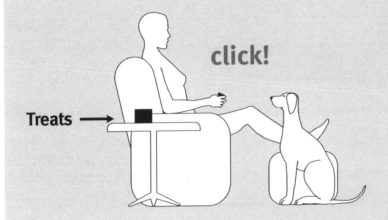

Treats

click!

TV

1. Click every time dog sits (no signals or talking)

2. Toss the treat past him so he has to get up to get it.

3. Repeat.

Sit: Shaping Method

Uses

Stopping jumping

Beginning of a stay

Some dogs are nervous about being in a vulnerable position and will not sit. Other dogs, like show dogs, are trained not to sit in the conformation show ring. Shaping is an excellent method for training skills that would be almost impossible to train with other methods. I first saw a shaping session at a Karen Pryor seminar. The wild puppy she used for a demonstration was sitting in three minutes. It was inspiring.

To shape a sit, watch your dog very carefully for the first signs of a sit. Don't give him any signals or talk to him. Click when he lowers his tail, moves his ears back, raises his head, or lowers his bottom even just an inch. Toss him the treat so he has to go get it. When he comes back, click as soon as he shows any sign of sitting again. Toss the treat again. Click and treat for the same movements several times. Then wait for a movement that is closer to your goal. Go slowly. Teach in several very short sessions (three to five minutes). Don't worry about your dog forgetting between sessions. Dogs don't forget what we have clicked. In fact, between sessions they may actually move a step closer to the actions we want (see *Latent Learning* on page 184.)

Begin adding a *cue* (see page 182) when he sits every time you have the clicker or treats.

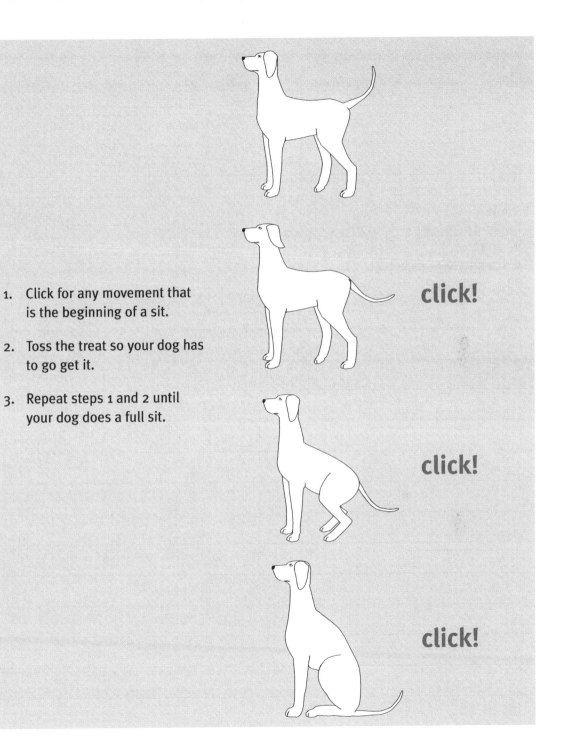

1. Click for any movement that is the beginning of a sit.

2. Toss the treat so your dog has to go get it.

3. Repeat steps 1 and 2 until your dog does a full sit.

click!

click!

click!

Magic Eyes

Uses

Keeping your dog's attention in spite of distractions

It is important that your dog learns to pay close attention to you. The following games make this skill fun and easy to teach.

Capture Method

Start this game by finding a quiet place. Every time your dog looks you in the eye, click and treat. Pretend the clicker is a camera shutter and you are taking a picture of your dog looking at your eyes.

After he starts looking at your eyes every time you have the clicker, go to more distracting places. Practice around children playing on skateboards. Play this game around other dogs or other distractions. Next, begin saying your *verbal cue* ("Watch me"or his name) just before you click. Gradually begin saying it when he is not watching you. Click and treat when he looks at you.

Magnet Method

Put a treat in one hand and the clicker in the other. Move the hand with the treat up to your eyes. When your dog looks up toward your eyes, click and give him the treat. After doing this about five times, move your hand to your eyes without the treat in it. Click and treat when your dog looks at your eyes.

You don't need to teach your dog a *verbal cue* with this method. Your hand motion becomes a *signal* to your dog.

See more information on cues on page 182.

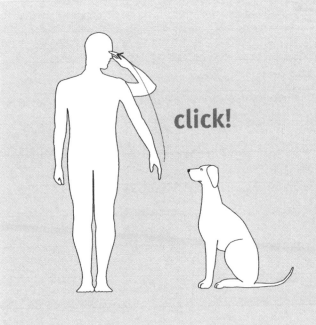

Capture Method

Click and treat when your dog looks at your eyes.

Magnet Method

1. Use food in your hand to lure your dog into looking at your eyes.

2. Click and treat.

3. After five repetitions use an empty hand.

Go to Your Mat: Shaping Method

This is an easy and fun way to teach your dog to settle in one spot. You simply click your dog as he gets closer to lying quietly on his mat. You can also use this game to teach him to go into his crate or get in a car. Follow these simple steps.

Uses

Eliminating begging at the table

Helping your dog to settle and be quiet

Showing your dog how to be a polite guest in other people's homes

1. Click your dog for looking or turning his head toward the mat. Treat.

2. Click for any movement toward the mat. Don't talk to him. Have him come to you to get his treat, so that he has to move back to the mat to get clicked again.

3. Continue clicking and treating. When he puts a paw on the mat, give him treats. See *Jackpot* on page 184.

4. If he gets stuck, expect less for a click (see *Going Back to Kindergarten,* page 187). Don't expect to get your dog on the mat in one session. Keep each training session short (three to five minutes).

5. After he has learned to settle on the mat, extend the time he stays before clicking and giving a treat.

6. Wait to add a *cue* (page 182) until he is going to the mat freely and staying there.

Hint: Give your dog a favorite bone or a Kong stuffed with dog treats (see Kongs, page 162) only when he is lying on his mat. Take it away if he moves off his mat. Give it back to him when he returns to his mat.

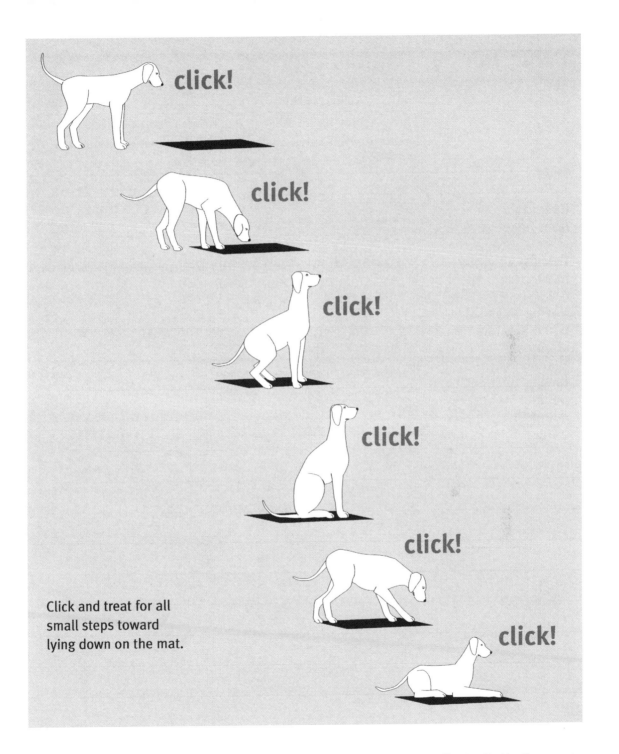

click!

click!

click!

click!

click!

Click and treat for all
small steps toward
lying down on the mat.

click!

Polite Puppy: Capture Method

This is a great way to ask your dog to sit. You *signal* (page 183) him by crossing your arms over your chest. Teach your dog to sit whenever people cross their arms and you will have a polite puppy.

Uses

Keeping dogs from jumping

Calming dogs by having them sit

Having dogs sit when greeting strangers

Having dogs sit politely before going through a door

1. Put a clicker in one hand and have treats nearby.

2. Make eye contact with your dog. Then dramatically fold your arms. Don't say "Sit."

3. If he sits, click and treat. Toss the treats to get him to stand up.

4. If he doesn't sit, move closer to him so he looks up to see you. This should lower his bottom.

5. If he jumps up on you, simply turn around until he stops jumping. Try again.

6. Ask friends to fold their arms. You click and treat when your dog sits.

7. After your dog learns to sit when you (or others) fold their arms, begin replacing the click with a *release word* (see page 186) such as "Release." Continue to give him treats for a good job.

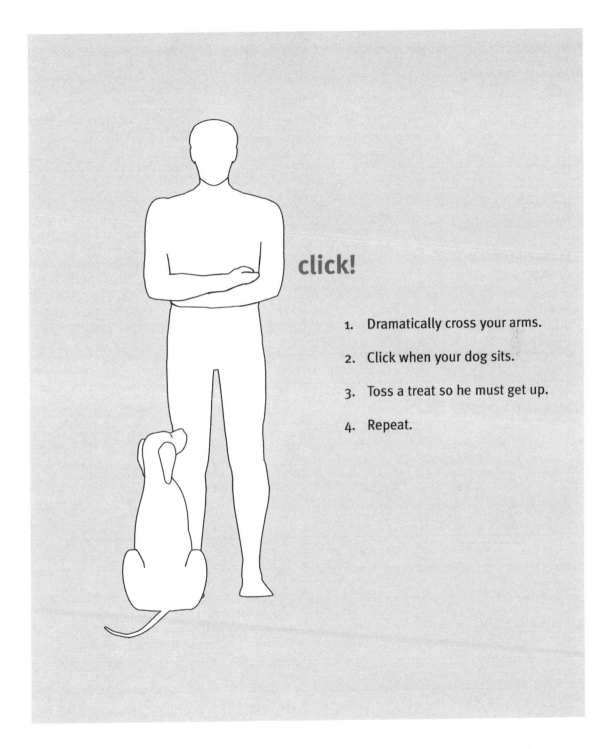

click!

1. Dramatically cross your arms.

2. Click when your dog sits.

3. Toss a treat so he must get up.

4. Repeat.

Loose Leash Walking: Make Like a Tree

Uses

Preventing injuries to your dog's neck

Preventing injuries to your body

Teaching your dog to pay attention to you

Does your dog pull you like a sled while you are trying to take him for a quiet walk? One reason for this pulling might be that you are unconsciously pulling back. We all pull back on something that is pulling us. Your dog works the same way. Every time you pull back on him, you are reinforcing his natural instincts to pull. Try this. Take an extra leash or belt and put it around your waist. Hook your dog's leash to the belt. Be careful that he does not trip you or pull you off balance. This works great with the clicker, because now you have your hands free for the clicker and treats. It also eliminates his tearing your shoulder out of its socket.

Start with your dog on your left side and the leash hanging slack. If your dog is truly walking on a loose leash, you should not feel any tension on the leash. When your dog starts to pull, bend your knees and make like a tree. Don't move or even look at your dog when he starts pulling. Don't pull back. Just stand there until the leash has some slack in it. When the leash is slack, click and treat and start moving forward again.

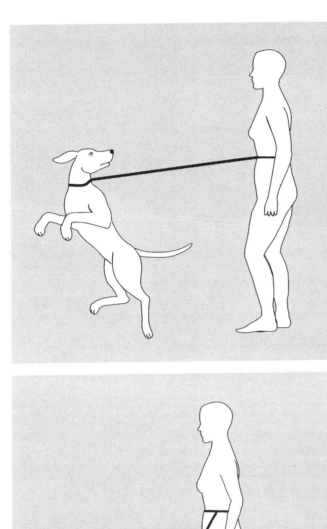

1. When your dog pulls, bend your knees, brace yourself, and stand still.

click!

2. When your dog stops pulling, click and treat and begin moving again.

Loose Leash Walking: Magnet Method

Teaching your dog to focus on you while walking on a leash

This game helps teach your dog to watch you instead of looking for cats or other dogs while you are out for a walk. This is a method that many animal trainers use. They call it ***targeting*** (see page 96 and 187). Your dog learns to focus on your left hand while you are walking.

Put your dog on your left side. Tie your dog's leash to your waist. This frees your hands for clicking and treating and prevents you from pulling on your dog's leash. Be careful not to trip on the leash. Put a treat in your left hand and hold it down in front of his nose. Walk three steps with the leash loose. Click if your dog is not pulling and stays on your left side. Open your hand and let him have the treat. Repeat another three steps. Click and treat. Gradually increase the number of steps that you can take without your dog pulling.

After you can walk fifteen feet without your dog pulling, put the treats in your pocket or close by and continue. If he begins pulling, start over but take fewer steps. Be sure to click before he begins to pull. Treat.

When your dog understands that he must stay on a loose leash, gradually introduce distractions. For example, if you have been working indoors, go out to your backyard. Don't expect to be able to take as many steps without him pulling when you change environments. Go back to three steps in the new place, then gradually add more steps again.

It is important to stop holding food in your hand. Food can become a ***bribe*** (see page 181). Keep food in your pocket or off your body entirely. Or, you can use a small toy and do a few seconds of play instead of a treat.

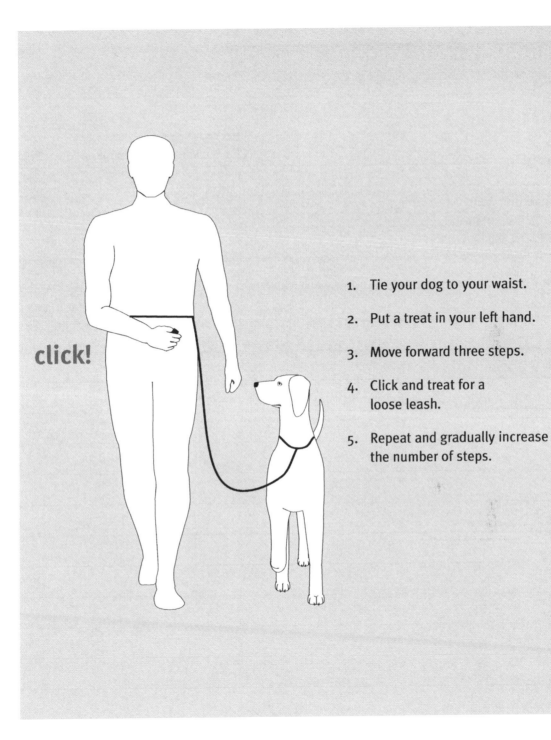

click!

1. Tie your dog to your waist.

2. Put a treat in your left hand.

3. Move forward three steps.

4. Click and treat for a loose leash.

5. Repeat and gradually increase the number of steps.

Loose Leash Walking: Penalty Yards

Uses

Teaching your dog not to pull on the leash

Clicker trainer Lana Mitchell uses this method to teach loose leash walking to a dog who is a confirmed puller.

Begin by selecting a start line. The line can be anything that will mark a starting point for you and your dog. Next, place something your dog wants (goal) about 20 feet away. This can be a treat, a person, or a toy. Keep your dog within three feet of your left side. I prefer to do this with my dog's leash tied to my waist. Let your dog know you are starting with a "Let's go." Walk toward the goal until he starts to pull. Immediately back up. Don't turn around and don't jerk him. Gently back up to the start line. Once you are back to the line, move forward again only when he is not pulling. Repeat going back to the start line until you can reach the goal without him pulling. When you both reach the goal with a loose leash, click and give him the goal object.

Even after your dog learns this game, he may still occasionally pull on the leash. If he does, stop and back up a few steps. Wait until he gets back into position and then continue your walk.

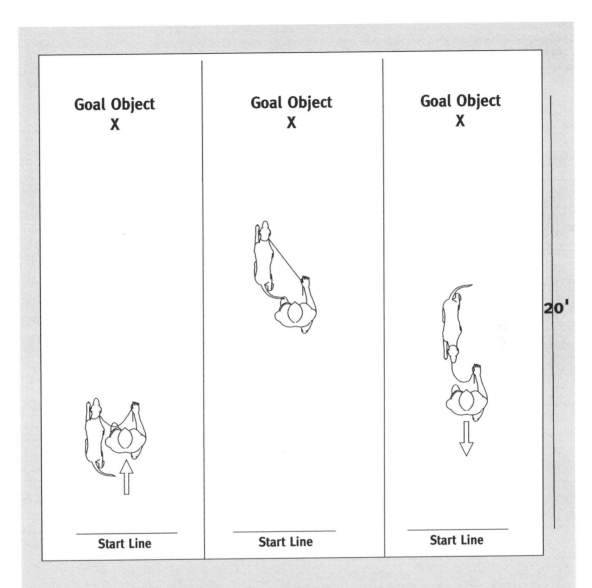

Goal Object
X

Goal Object
X

Goal Object
X

20'

Start Line

Start Line

Start Line

1. Walk toward the goal object until your dog starts pulling.

2. When your dog starts pulling, back up to the start line.

3. When he gets to the goal without pulling, click and let him have the goal object.

Catch Me Game

Uses

**Teaching your
dog to stay close
to your side
when off leash**

This game will help you teach your dog that walking close to you is fun and rewarding.

Find a safe place and take your dog off his leash. You can begin this game in your house. Hold the clicker in your right hand and have lots of treats in your pockets or nearby. Start walking around without looking, calling, or hinting to your dog. Click and treat when he comes into position at your left side. Turn and walk in the opposite direction if he runs past you. If he wanders away, keep walking but click and treat him for coming toward you. Keep clicking and treating for him getting closer to the walking position at your left side.

Warning: Do this in a fenced or enclosed space. Dogs should always be on a leash when there is any possibility that they could get hurt. Having your dog off the leash is also often illegal. You could be fined for a loose dog, even if he is well behaved.

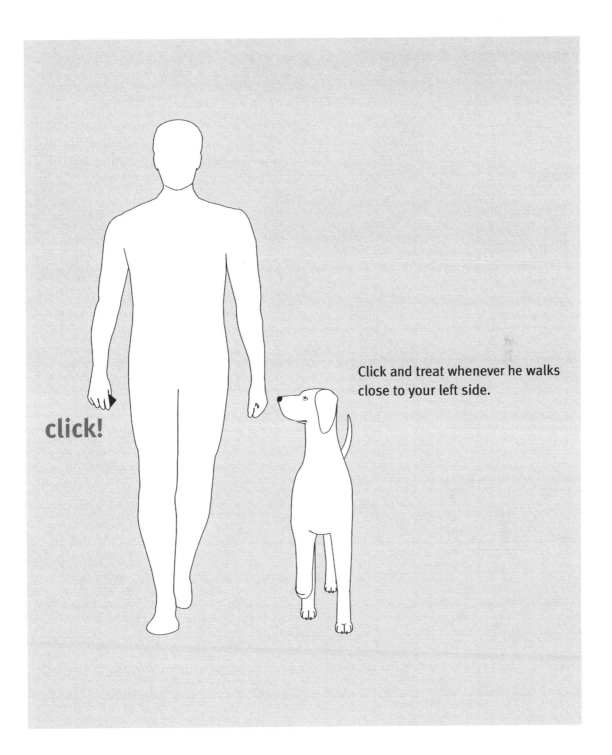

click!

Click and treat whenever he walks close to your left side.

Ping-Pong Puppy: Coming When Called

Teaching your dog to come every time you call

Saving your dog's life

Start with two or more people sitting (or standing) six feet apart. Have everyone take turns calling your dog and giving him a treat. Everyone should use the same word ("Here" or "Come") and be sure to use a happy voice tone. Each person should click and treat when the puppy touches them. As your dog learns to come, increase the distance. You can see an example of this on Karen Pryor's *Clicker Magic* video (see page 194).

Here is another game. Put cups of treats in every room. Every time you call your dog, give him a treat for coming even if you don't have your clicker. Make the treats small. Be sure you always call your dog with the same word. If he doesn't come when you call, smile and bend down with arms outstretched, wide and welcome. If he still does not come, back up quickly. Never call your dog for bad things. Don't call your dog to come in from play; instead, go get him. Don't call your dog and then lock him up for the day. Do call him for fun things (dinner, a walk, a game).

When he is always coming indoors, go outside. Start calling him again from only six feet and gradually increase the distance.

I know of one dog who came when called. Just before the owner could put a hand on his collar he ran into the street and was killed by a car. Every time you call your dog have him come and touch you. Then gently take his collar while giving him a treat. If your dog does not allow you to place your hand on his collar, practice with the clicker and treats. Teach him to come closer to you until you can quickly grab his collar anytime you wish.

Note: The clicker is a very powerful tool. Don't misuse it by clicking to attract your dog's attention. Never click unless your dog is doing the exact action you want.

1. Begin calling your dog from six feet.

2. Always give a treat when he comes. Put your hand on his collar before you give the treat.

3. Gradually increase the distance.

4. Gradually increase the distractions.

Hide-and-Go-Seek: Coming When Called

Teaching your dog to come happily when called

This is a fun way to teach your dog to come to you. Kids love this. Have someone gently hold your dog in one room of the house. Hide in another room. Your first hiding places should be very easy. Make it easy for your dog to succeed at first. Call him with the word you have chosen ("Here" or "Come"). When he finds you, welcome him warmly. Put your hand on his collar, click and give him a treat. Children should learn not to run away from him. As an added safeguard for small children, you should teach your dog to sit before the child gives him a treat.

After your dog is coming every time, start hiding in more difficult places and farther away. Next, go outside and play the game in a safe, enclosed environment.

1. Hide (make it easy at first).

2. Call your dog with your special word for coming.

3. Put your hand on his collar. Click and give him a treat.

Down: Capture Method

Uses

Prevent barking

Keep your dog safe

This is the easiest way to teach your dog to lie down. You can do it while having your morning cup of coffee or while doing other daily activities. Watch your dog carefully. Any time your dog lies down on his own, click and treat him. Don't talk to him or give him any signal, just wait until he lies down. After you click, toss a treat so that he must get up to get it. After he has lain down several times, change your position, or start again later in a new place. When you are sure he understands he must lie down to get a click, extend the time he is down. Begin by adding just a few seconds between the time he lies down and the time you click. Start adding a *verbal cue* (see page 182) when he begins to lie down and look at you, expecting a click and a treat.

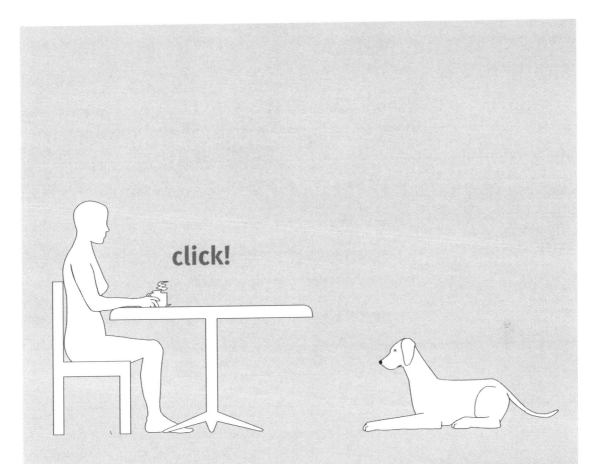

click!

Click and treat when your dog chooses to lie down on his own.

Down: Magnet Method

Stopping jumping

Beginning of a stay

Start with your dog in a sit position. Hold a treat in your hand. Put it very close to your dog's nose. Slowly move your hand down to the floor. Make sure your hand goes down between your dog's front paws. If at first your dog does not want to lie down all the way, you can click for as far down as he will go. You may need to click and treat him for just looking down. Continue with very small steps and click and treat often until you have him going all the way down. Click as soon he is down, then toss the treat to get him up. After your dog goes all the way down five times, remove the treat from your hand and have him follow your empty hand.

Your hand motion will become a ***hand signal*** (see page 183) to your dog. When he lies down every time on your hand signal you may start adding a ***verbal cue*** (see page 182) like "Down" just as you give him the signal.

click!

Use food to lure your dog into the down position.

Stay

You need to teach your dog stay in two stages. These stages are distance and time. Begin working on distance first by moving away from your dog while he stays. Don't have him stay more than a few seconds.

Uses

Teaching dogs to stay at doors (prevents dogs from running out of the house)

Waiting safely in the car until released to come out

Greeting people or other dogs calmly

Staying while you go up or down stairs

1. Have your dog sit (or lie down) next to you.
2. Say "Stay" only once or use a ***hand signal*** (page 183).
3. Take one step away from him.
4. Click and treat. He can move after the click.
5. If your dog moves before you click, go back and start over.
6. Repeat several times.
7. Next move away one more step and click and treat.
8. Repeat moving away from your dog one step at a time. When you can move six feet from him and he stays, begin working on lengthening the time he stays.
9. Have him sit (or lie down).
10. Say "Stay" (only once) and move away six feet.
11. Click and treat after ten seconds. Click only if he stays.
12. Gradually increase the time and repeat. After your dog is staying for a minute or two, you may start increasing your distance from him again. If he becomes confused, either move closer or shorten the time he stays.

The click always ends the game. It is a release, so your dog can move after you click. If you want to teach a ***release word*** (see page 186), click while giving the release word. This pairs the click with the word. Gradually decrease the click but continue the release word and the treat.

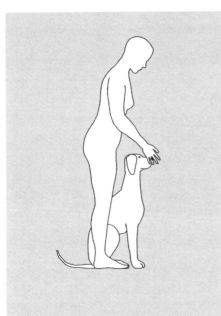

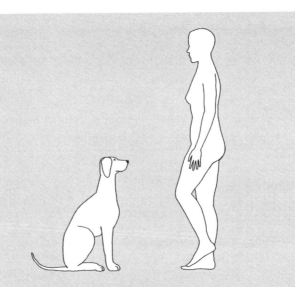

1. Signal your dog to stay.

2. Move away from him one step.
3. Click and treat if he stays.
4. Increase your distance but not the time.

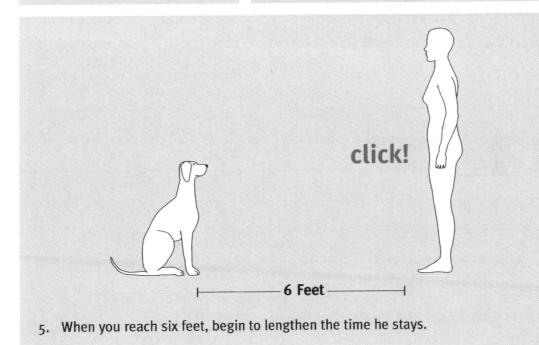

click!

|— 6 Feet —|

5. When you reach six feet, begin to lengthen the time he stays.

Strengthening the Stay

**Waiting patiently
to be fed**

**Waiting to have
his leash put on**

When your dog understands how to stay, you can strengthen his stay by asking him to stay while you put his food down at mealtimes. Have him hold the stay for only a couple seconds at first. Then give him your release word and allow him to eat. No click or treat is necessary.

You can also have him do a short stay before going out for a walk. Ask for a stay while you hook his leash onto his collar. Click or give a release word and go out the door. You can also teach him to stay before getting in or out of the car.

The last part of teaching a good stay is to add distractions. Distractions can be kids playing, food, new environments, or other dogs. Begin by standing close to your dog. Click for very short stays in the presence of distractions. Gradually increase the distance and time. Don't expect too much too soon.

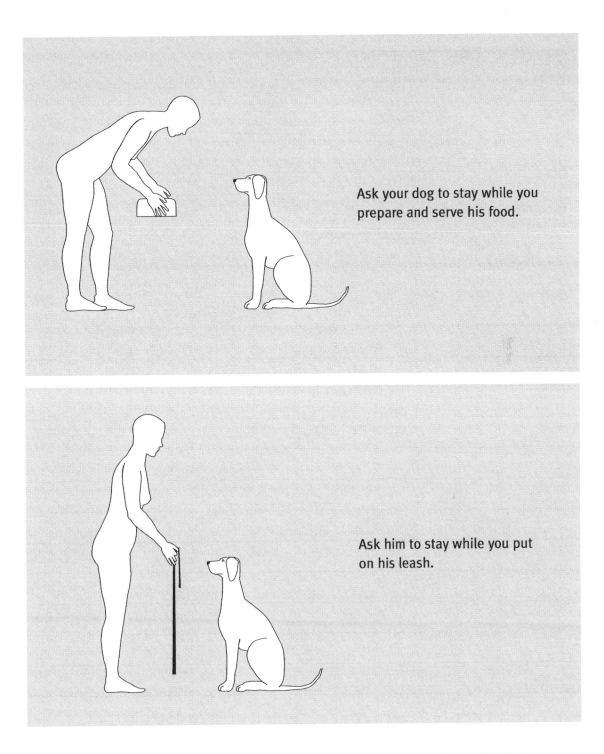

Ask your dog to stay while you prepare and serve his food.

Ask him to stay while you put on his leash.

Stand: The Magnet Method

Uses

Grooming

**Allowing veteri-
narian checks**

Stopping jumping

Animal behaviorists use the stand to teach animals to allow handling for vet exams, grooming and other care (see page 88). A dog who is in a standing position, with all four feet on the floor, cannot be jumping on you or your guests.

To teach the stand, have your dog sit in front of you. Put a treat in your right hand. Put your clicker in your left hand. Hold your hand with the food in it very close to your dog's nose. Slowly move your hand away from his nose. Your food hand should look as if it is pulling your dog into a stand. As soon as he is standing, click and treat. Even if your dog does not immediately move to a stand, click and treat for any movement toward a stand.

When your dog stands for you every time, put the food on a table away from you and repeat your hand movement without food in your hand. Your hand movement will then become your *signal* (see page 183) for a stand.

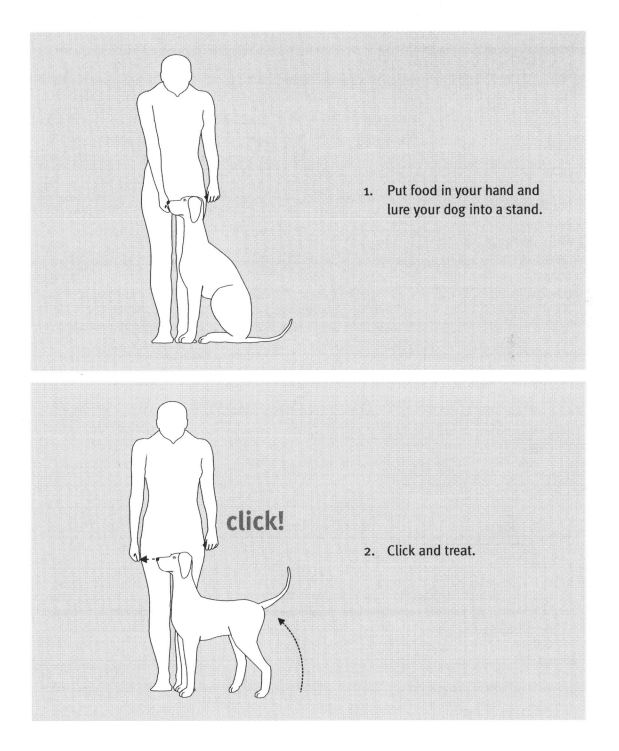

1. Put food in your hand and lure your dog into a stand.

click!

2. Click and treat.

Doggie Zen

Uses

Stopping begging

Stop hand biting

Teaching self-control

This is a great way to show your canine friend that pushing and being a bully won't get what he wants. He learns that to get what he wants he must give it up first. This is the first step to teaching dogs to "Leave it."

Start by finding a great treat that your dog loves. Make sure he knows you have the treat in your hand. Close your hand around the treat. Put your hand low enough for him to reach your hand. Allow him to try to get the treat from you. He can push, nibble, or lick. When he gives up (looks away or backs away), click and open your hand for him to take the treat.

Don't say anything to your dog when you first start this game. After he understands he will not get a treat by being pushy, begin giving him a release word (like "Take it") as you open your hand.

Stop playing the game if he starts to get pushy. Don't say anything, just put the treat away and ignore your dog. If your dog becomes aggressive, you should consult a qualified ***animal behaviorist*** (see page 180) for help.

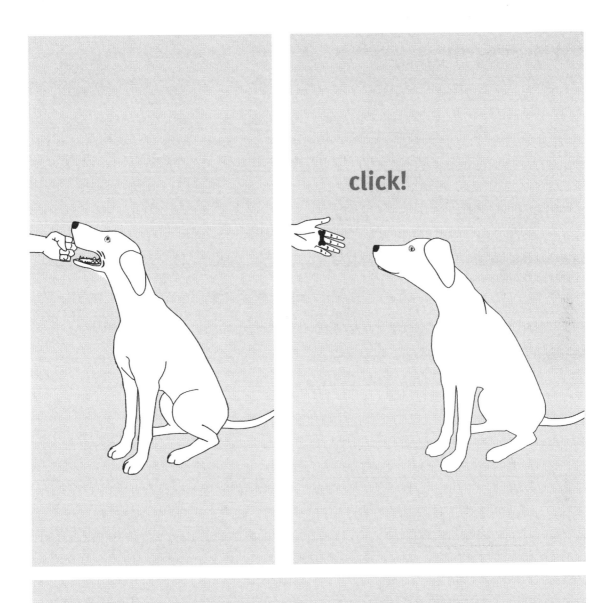

click!

Give it up to get it!
Give your dog the treat only when he stops trying to take it.

Leave It: (Part I)

Uses

Saving your dog from danger

Protecting your possessions or food

Ignoring cats, dogs, and other distractions

"Leave it" is a very important skill for your dog. Dogs often grab items that could injure or kill them. Grabbing stuff can also just make your life miserable. Dogs can run away with your socks while you are dressing or find a lovely skunk just as you are planning to go out for the evening.

Animal behaviorist Kathy Sdao introduced me to this method for teaching your dog to "Leave it." First teach your dog the Doggie Zen game (page 60). Continue the game by lowering the treat in small steps to the floor. Close your hand if your dog attempts to get the treat. When your dog looks away or backs up, click and open your hand while saying your release word. Continue this until your hand is on the floor.

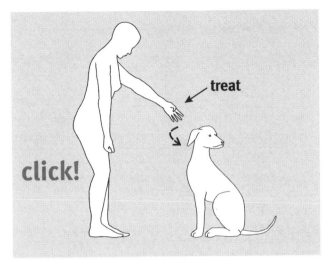

click!

treat

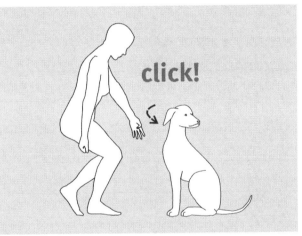

click!

1. Click and give the treat to
   the dog when he looks away
   or backs up.

2. Lower the treat in small
   steps toward the floor.

3. At each stage, click and
   give the treat to the dog
   when he looks away or
   backs up.

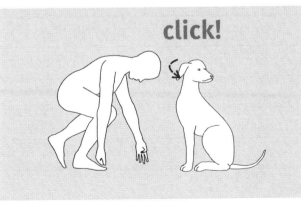

click!

Leave It: (Part 2)

Gradually begin placing the treat directly on the floor and then stand up. If your dog tries to grab the treat, cover it with your foot. When your dog looks away or backs up instead of trying to get the treat, click and uncover the treat. Allow him to eat the treat.

Begin adding the ***verbal cue*** "Leave it." To do this, say the words "Leave it" as your dog backs up or looks away (see page 182 for more information on cues).

Next, put the treat in different places. Require your dog to wait for a click or ***release word*** (see page 186) before you allow him to take it. Practice this in many different locations. If your dog tries to take the treat without permission, re-teach the game in the new location (see ***Going Back to Kindergarten,*** page 187).

You can use the words "Leave it" when your dog wants something that has been dead for a month, finds a skunk, or grabs something off the floor. I am sure you will find many uses for this game.

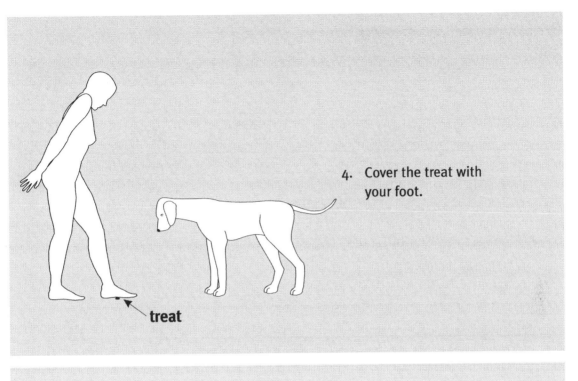

4. Cover the treat with your foot.

treat

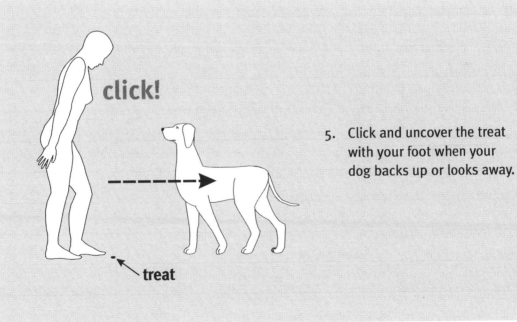

click!

treat

5. Click and uncover the treat with your foot when your dog backs up or looks away.

Chapter 4
Other Practical Skills

The Give Game

All dogs must learn to give up items. You should not try to force your dog to give up any item. Doing this could make him more possessive and could even be dangerous.

To teach your dog to give up an item, begin by teaching him to trade what he has for something you have. Give your dog a toy. While he is playing with the toy, offer him either a favorite food treat or a favorite toy. The minute he drops his toy to take your item, click and give it to him. Once he gets the idea, begin saying "Give" as you click.

Continue teaching him with the clicker to put the object in your hand. First click him for dropping it close to your hand. Then begin clicking for drops closer to your hand. Click and give a big *jackpot* (see page 184) of treats when he puts it into your hand.

If your dog grabs an object and starts to run off, daring you to chase him, offer him a trade. If he shows no interest in your toy, make it more interesting by playing with it yourself. Pretend that you don't want him to have your toy.

Avoid making this game into a *bribe* (see page 181). When your dog is giving up his item freely, don't show him your trade item. Make it a surprise reward instead.

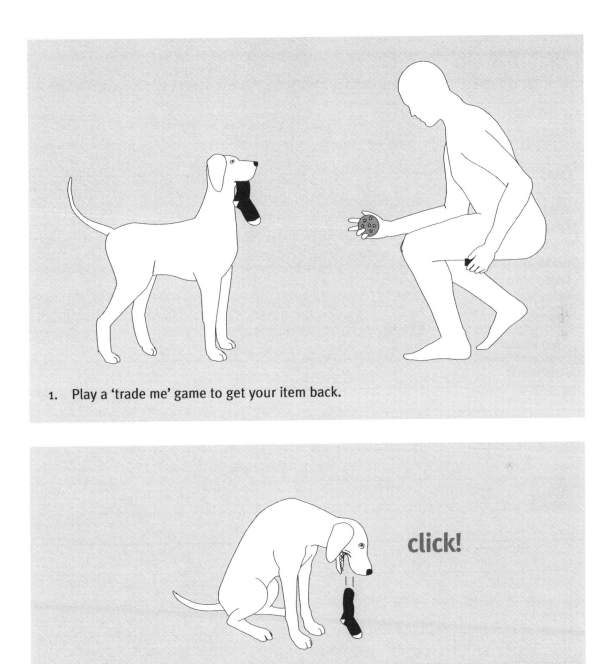

1. Play a 'trade me' game to get your item back.

click!

2. Click and give him a treat when he drops it.

Picking Up Items

Teaching how to play with new toys

Overcoming fear of new objects

Some dogs don't like to pick things up or even to play with toys. It is important your dog learns to pick up objects. He can then learn how to retrieve.

If your dog is not interested in picking up items, use this shaping method to teach him how much fun it is to retrieve and play with toys. First, make the toy more desirable by rubbing peanut butter or cheese on it. When your dog licks, sniffs, or even looks at the object, click and treat. Repeat clicking and treating several times for licking or sniffing.

Next, click and treat when he touches the toy with his mouth or lips. Click him for touching it with his teeth. Continue clicking and treating for any action toward your goal of him picking up the object. Go slow and keep the sessions short.

Be sure to play with your dog and the item.

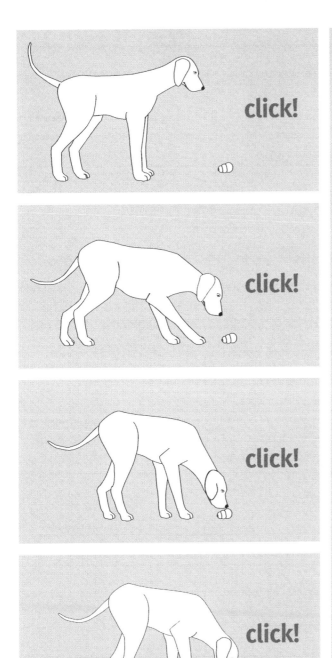

1. Click your dog for looking at the item.

2. Have him come to you to get the treat.

3. Click each time he gets closer to the item.

4. Click him for touching it.

5. Click him for putting the item in his mouth.

Get It Game 1

Uses

Picking up items you drop (pencils, papers, and keys)

Most dogs love to chase and catch moving objects. This makes this game very easy to teach. This is the beginning of teaching your dog how to retrieve items for you.

First, toss treats on the floor one at a time. Just as you toss the treat (only a few feet away at first) say "Get it" or another **verbal cue** (see page 182). Start tossing the treats farther away. Next, start tossing a toy or rolling a ball instead of the treat.

Some dogs will not even pay attention to a toy. If this happens, click your dog for even looking in the direction of the toy. Give a treat and continue clicking him for getting closer to the toy. Then click for touching the toy. Then click for putting his mouth on the toy. Follow every click with a treat. Be sure to go slow and do as many sessions as you need to get him to pick up the toy.

After your dog is picking up the toy, begin clicking and treating him for coming to you with it. Do this in baby steps the same way you did for getting him to pick it up.

Some dogs will bring the toy to you if you step back away from him. You can even run away from him (children shouldn't do this). Make a really big fuss when your dog comes to you with the toy. Use the clicker Give Game (page 68) to swap the toy for a treat while saying "Give." Toss it again if he is still interested in the game. Do this only a few times per session.

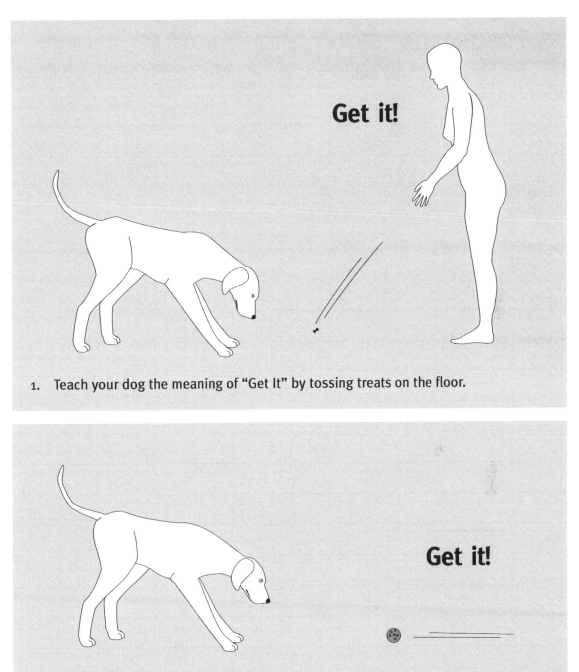

Get it!

1. Teach your dog the meaning of "Get It" by tossing treats on the floor.

Get it!

2. Then begin switching the treats for fun toys.

Get It Game 2

Teaching a retrieve

Supplying mental exercise

Supplying physical exercise

Have a friend stand six feet away from you and your dog. Have your friend wave an exciting toy. Gently hold your dog until he shows that he wants to go get the toy, then let go of him. Be sure your friend does not play with him or let him pull on the toy. When your dog gets the toy, excitedly call him back to you. Praise and play with him and the toy. Swap the toy for a treat while saying "Give" (see game on page 68). Repeat the game. Next, increase the distance.

After your dog is coming back to you with his toy, have your friend put the toy on the floor. Let your dog get it and bring it back to you. When he will bring the toy back to you, start rolling or tossing it for him to retrieve.

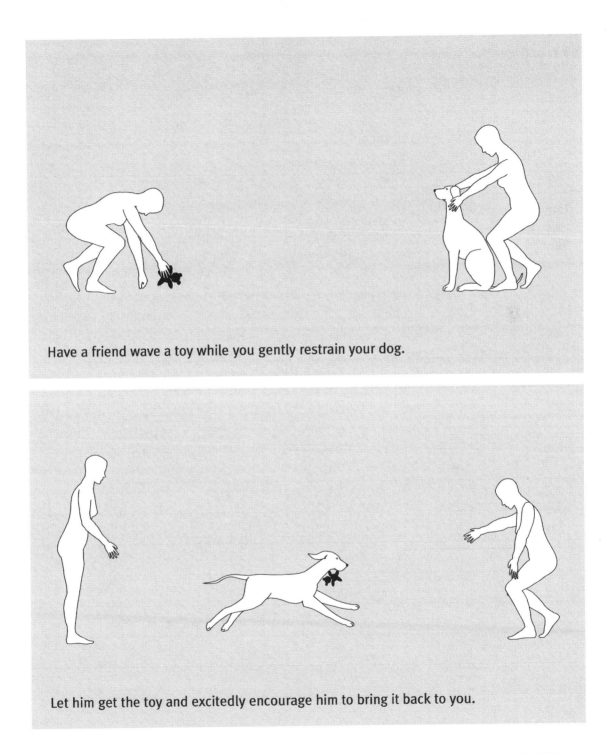

Have a friend wave a toy while you gently restrain your dog.

Let him get the toy and excitedly encourage him to bring it back to you.

Find It Game

Uses

Teaches finding and retrieving objects

I can never remember where I left my slippers. So I trained my dog to go find them and bring them to me. Here's how to teach your dog to find and bring you items.

Begin by teaching your dog to find a favorite toy. Have him sit and stay. If needed, you can have someone stay with him. Move away from your dog. Put the toy down (at first in plain sight). Go back to your dog and tell him to "Find it." Run with him to get the toy. Then race back to the starting point. Play with him at the starting point. Swap the toy for a treat while saying "Give," and repeat the game. Make the toy more difficult to find. Begin staying closer to the starting point, so he has to bring it back to you. Eventually you can ask him to stay and go to another room to hide the toy. Return and tell him to "Find it." He will find it and bring it back to you.

Once your dog learns the 'Find it Game' you can begin teaching him to find any dog-safe item. Teach the name of the article you want your dog to retrieve. I began by pointing at my slippers and saying "Find it" and "Slippers." I then gave my dog a big click and treat when he gave me my slippers.

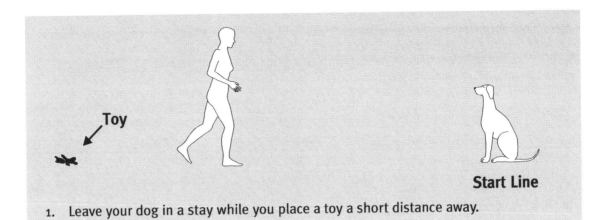

Toy

1. Leave your dog in a stay while you place a toy a short distance away.

Start Line

2. Release him and say "Find it." Run with him to get the toy.

Start Line

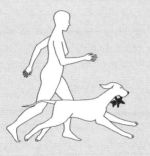

3. Run back to the start line before asking your dog for the toy. Reward him by playing with him and the toy.

Start Line

Crate Training

**Giving your dog
a safe den**

**Helping house
training**

A crate is has advantages for both humans and dogs. Teach your dog that his crate is his safe den by playing this clicker game with him.

1. Take off the crate's door or tie it open.
2. Click if your dog even looks at the crate. Have him come back to you to get his treat.
3. Click and treat him for taking one step toward the crate. Then for two steps. Then for three steps. Be sure to have him return to you for a treat after every click.
4. Click and give a big treat *jackpot* (see page 184) when he touches the crate.
5. Continue clicking and treating until he puts his head in the crate.
6. Click and treat for each foot he puts in the crate. Be sure to have him come back to you for his treat.
7. When he goes all the way into the crate, give a click and give him a big jackpot. Be sure to allow him to come back out.
8. Begin delaying your clicks (only a few seconds at a time) to encourage him to stay inside the crate. Don't rush him as he learns to stay. Click and treat only for going into the crate, never click as he is coming out.
9. Click if he sits or lies down in the crate. Give him a treat or another jackpot.

Don't rush your dog. He may need several sessions to accomplish the nine steps listed above. You may need to repeat some steps for several sessions before he goes into the crate on his own. Always allow him to come out whenever he wishes.

When your dog is voluntarily sitting or lying down in his crate, you can slowly begin the process of closing the door. At first close the door for just a few seconds, then click and toss in a treat. Very slowly increase the time the door is closed.

After your dog considers the crate his private spot, begin teaching him a *verbal cue* (see page 182) for going into his crate.

Click and treat for every small step toward your dog going into his crate on his own.

Be sure to have him return to you after every click for his treat.

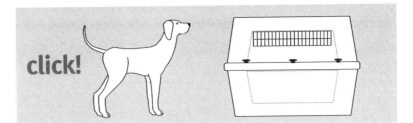

click!

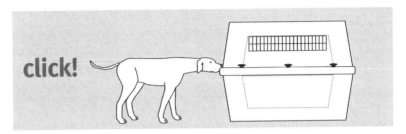

click!

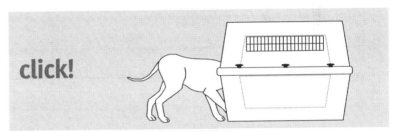

click!

click!

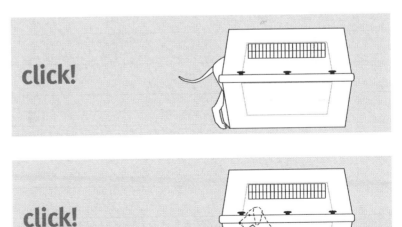

click!

House Training

Uses

House training without losing your puppy's trust

Teaching a special potty spot

Teaching a 'potty' cue

If your puppy came from a knowledgeable breeder, his mother may have already trained him to eliminate outside. If the breeder provided a way for the mother dog to take her puppies out, the mother dog will often house train her puppies. However, if you're reading this, you probably have to do house training yourself. Your goal is to teach your puppy the right place to eliminate.

The first thing you must do is choose one spot that will be his permanent bathroom. When the puppy has an accident in the house (and he will), remain as calm as possible. If you're lucky you will catch him before he finishes. Quietly go get the puppy and take him out to his potty spot. Click and treat and play with him as soon as he eliminates there. He should learn: potty in house = no reward; potty in potty spot = really great rewards!

Quietly say a word that will be a cue to tell your dog that this is the place and time to go. Be careful in choosing your 'potty' word. You will want to use this word in public. This cue will come in very handy when you're away from home.

Go back into the house and use paper towels to pick up the mistake. Place the towels in the potty spot. Leave the towels there as a signal to your dog that this is the correct place for him to eliminate. Don't let the place get dirty, just leave enough to mark the spot for your puppy.

Clean up the area your puppy used by mistake with white vinegar. Vinegar will help eliminate the odor. You can also buy products at pet stores to help remove the odor. Removal of the odor is important in discouraging the puppy from using that spot again.

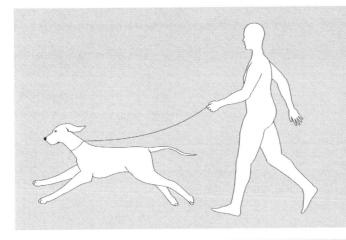

Watch your puppy. When he needs to go, take him to the same chosen 'potty' spot.

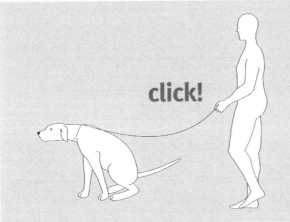

click!

Say your 'potty' word when he begins to go and then click.

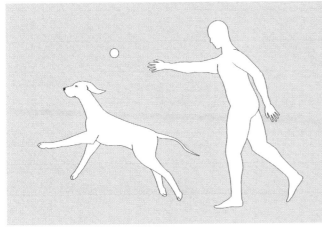

After he finishes, make a big fuss over him and reward him with a treat or play.

Bell Signal

Giving your dog a way to signal you that he needs to go out

A bell can be a useful tool for your dog to tell you he wants to go out. Because he can't speak to you in your language, he must use a signal to tell you he needs to go out. You must learn to recognize that signal. I put a bell on the door that leads to the potty spot. The bell rings every time someone goes in or out that door. Remember how fast a dog learns what a doorbell means? Well, your puppy will learn that the bell means that the door is opening. Many puppies will go to the bell and ring it without any special training. However, to speed up the process, take him to the bell. If he touches it, click and treat him. Then quickly open the door and run outside, praising him. If he shows no interest in touching the bell, you can rub cheese or peanut butter on it.

Put a bell on the door and teach him to ring it when he needs to go out

House Training Management

Making house training easy and natural

If you understand when your puppy needs to go out, then you can eliminate many accidents. The following suggestions will help your puppy succeed with his house training.

1. Always watch the puppy. You can tie the puppy to you in the house. You can confine the puppy to the room you are in with puppy gates. You can also crate train him (see page 78).
2. Feed on a fixed schedule. Usually he will need to go right after he has eaten.
3. Always take him out after eating, playing, any excitement. He will need to go out after exercise, after waking up, and before going to bed at night.

When you take your puppy out to potty, always use the same door and go to the same potty spot. Plan on waiting for him. Let him sniff around before he goes. When he begins going, quietly say your potty *cue* (see page 80 for more information on house training).

If he doesn't eliminate, go back inside and try again later. When he does go, click, make a fuss over him and reward him with a treat or play.

It is a good idea to put the puppy in a crate at night. Most puppies don't want to eliminate in their nest. If your puppy is very small and you have a large crate, divide it up so the puppy has just enough room to stand up and turn around. Depending on the age of the puppy, you may have to get up in the middle of the night to take him out. I found by putting the crate in my bedroom at night I could hear my puppy wake up. I could then take him out before he eliminated in his crate. Always take the puppy out when you first get up in the morning.

If your puppy has an accident, try not to be angry or upset (I know this is hard), because if he fears you it will slow his learning process. This is not an instant process, but if it's done properly your dog won't fear you and he will learn what you want.

Take Your Puppy Out Immediately	
After	feeding
After	drinking water
After	waking up from a nap
After	playing
After	clicker sessions
After	any excitement (dogs, people, or toys)
After	being in his crate
After	waking up in the morning
Before	going to bed at night

Car Riding

A dog who rides nicely in the car is a pleasure. Dogs are company on long lonely trips. Dogs also don't criticize your driving.

This is what I would recommend for your puppy's first trip. Have a passenger hold the puppy. The passenger should protect his clothing with a soft towel (bring extras). If no one is available to help you, then put the puppy in a small crate. Use the seat belts to strap in the crate. (Check with your car's manufacturer about possible air bag dangers.) If possible, at stop lights put your finger in the crate and talk to the puppy. Make it a pleasant, short experience.

After a few trips, begin putting the crate in the back seat or begin using a doggie seat belt. If you have a small dog, you can buy a booster seat with a built-in safety belt.

Seat belts or crates not only keep your dog safe, but can also teach him to ride politely in the car. He cannot charge around the car barking at everything that goes by. Most dogs will simply curl up and go to sleep. Give your dog a stuffed Kong or a chew toy if he seems restless.

If you have an adult dog who hates to ride in a car, use your clicker to help him overcome his fear (see *systematic desensitization* on page 187). Begin by encouraging him to get in and out of the car. Click and treat him for jumping in the car. When he seems happy to get in the car, begin slowly getting him used to his seat belt or crate while the car is running but not moving. Click and treat each step and do it in many sessions. Your first trip should be just around the block with a big treat at the end.

An important skill to teach your dog is to "Stay" (see page 54) in the car until you give him a *release word* (see page 186) to get out.

Be very careful about leaving your dog alone in the car, even for a short time. A car can heat up quickly, and could kill your dog. Also, open windows can tempt children to put their hands in the car. Your dog might attempt to protect your car by biting.

Dog seat belts help restrain and calm your dog. They keep him safer in an accident.

Handling: (Animal Husbandry)

Uses

Grooming

Veterinarian visits

A requirement for some dog sports and activities

Dog trainers call exercises that teach animals useful skills for future veterinary treatment or routine grooming 'handling exercises.' Zookeepers and marine mammal trainers use the term 'husbandry training.'

Kathy Sdao, MA, an animal behaviorist who owns Bright Spot Dog Training in Tacoma, Washington, explains the benefits of training your dog to allow handling:

"Vets, vet techs and groomers would be happier and safer. Dogs would be way less stressed. And, owners would have more options for managing the health of their dogs, and they might even have less expensive vet bills. For example, one of my dogs popped some post-operative stitches on her chest last year. Because she'd been trained to 'freeze,' or hold still in any position, my vet and I were able to ask her to do this on the exam table. Dr. Lisa stapled the wound, thereby saving the time, expense, and invasiveness of re-anesthetizing an eleven-year old dog."

Kathy suggests you teach your dog to:
- Get in a tub and stand for a bath
- Present paws for nail trims
- Allow teeth-cleaning
- Swallow pills
- Tolerate brushing
- Remain calm (i.e., desensitization) for injections and blood draws

You can teach all the above items by clicking for any movement toward the action you want. For example, to teach your dog to allow you to clean his teeth, begin by teaching him that it's okay for you to handle his face. Click and treat him for letting you get close, for light touching, for lifting his lips, and finally for touching his teeth.

If you have a young puppy, begin by playing with all parts of his body. Look at his teeth, play with his tail, his ears, his feet, and roll his loose skin gently between your fingers. Do anything that doesn't scare him. Be sure to make it a game. Have strangers do the same things. Follow all this handling with a treat or play. Take your puppy to see the vet just to get acquainted. Have the vet give him a treat. Visit the groomers, have them give him a treat. The more positive handling you do with your puppy, the more accepting he will be of new experiences as an adult dog.

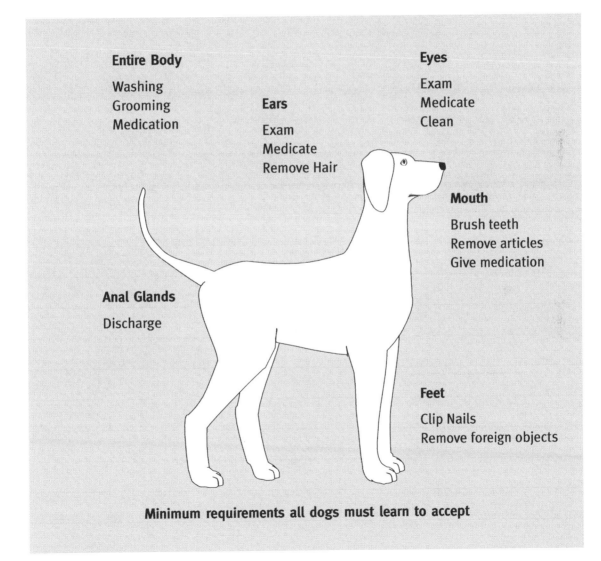

Entire Body

Washing
Grooming
Medication

Ears

Exam
Medicate
Remove Hair

Eyes

Exam
Medicate
Clean

Mouth

Brush teeth
Remove articles
Give medication

Anal Glands

Discharge

Feet

Clip Nails
Remove foreign objects

Minimum requirements all dogs must learn to accept

Chapter 5
Useful Tricks and Games

Teaching Useful Tricks

Many people seem to think that teaching dog tricks is a frivolous waste of time. However, dogs love learning tricks. Patty Ruzzo, author and dog trainer, says "There is no such thing as obedience training . . . it is all about tricks."

Dogs are great game players. Everything is a trick or game to dogs. Unfortunately, we often don't view what our new puppy is doing as a game. When we find our favorite jacket chewed and in the mud, it's hard to remember that your new puppy just saw this as a wonderful new toy. We need to invent useful games for our dogs before they invent games that we might not like.

Besides redirecting your dog's energy you can gain other benefits from teaching tricks to your dog.

Why To Teach Tricks

1. **Create a helpful dog.** Dogs who know useful tricks can work for us. They see it as a fun game. For example, many people have taught their dogs to find their keys. You can see how useful this trick could be if you dropped your keys in the mud or deep snow.

2. **Improve your teaching abilities.** Tricks help you learn how to teach your dog. Teaching a trick can build your confidence in your teaching ability and it takes the pressure off you and your dog. Everyone has fun.

3. **Have fun.** Everyone learns faster when they're having fun. We loosen up, laugh and smile a lot when we are teaching a dog to spin. We get stern and serious when we teach something like "Stay." Dogs are sensitive to our moods. Test this out by smiling and laughing at your dog and see how he reacts.

4. **Safety.** Tricks can help show children how to play safely with a dog. This is one of my favorite ways to use tricks. Even the most well behaved dog can accidentally injure a child who does not understand how to act around dogs. Young children can unintentionally hurt a dog by grabbing an ear or pulling fur. The dog might react by trying to protect himself. To avoid this problem I use tricks like High Five, Sit Up, and Spin. When children ask to play with my dog, I ask if they would like to see his tricks. I ask the children to stand back while he does his tricks. Then instead of letting the children pet my dog, I show them how to cue or signal him to do a trick. Children of all ages love to be able to ask a dog to do a trick.

5. **Increase your dog's learning ability.** Learning for dogs is just like learning for people. The more we learn the easier it becomes. Your dog learns that he can get a reward if he understands your signals and cues. Then he'll catch on more quickly when you are teaching other skills.

Capture Something Cute

Uses

Teaching you how to clicker train

Helping dogs learn

Providing a safe way for children to play with your dog

Having fun

This is an easy way to learn how to begin to teach your dog a trick. Watch your dog carefully and pick an action he does naturally. It could be a cute head tilt, or the way he lies upside down, or even the way he smiles.

To capture the action you want to train, click at the exact second that he does it. Then give him a treat. Your dog most likely will not repeat the action right away. Don't worry, simply wait until he does the same thing again, then click and treat.

If you don't have a clicker with you when you notice him doing his 'cute' game, then enthusiastically say a word like "Yessssss!" Then give him his treat. After catching this cute action several times, you may notice that he is repeating it more often. When he walks up to you and begins his cute game to get your attention, it's time to teach him a name for it. Put it on a *verbal cue*. Pick a funny name. Or, use a hand *signal* that you can gradually make so small that people won't see you signaling your dog (see more information about cues on page 182). Now ask him to do the trick whenever you feel like showing off his special cuteness.

Capturing a cute trick will improve your timing and confidence. It will also help your dog learn that being with you is really fun. Have fun teaching this game.

click!

Click and give a treat every time your dog does something cute that you'd like to see again.

Target Stick/Targeting: (Part 1)

Uses

Leading your dog's movements without force

A tool for teaching other useful skills

Having fun

Teaching attention

This is the first thing I taught my dog with the clicker. I couldn't even wait until the second day of the clicker training seminar I was attending. I had to try it right away. I took a stick and held it out for my five-month-old puppy to see. He came right over and touched it with his nose. I clicked and gave him a treat. Over the next few days we repeated this process. Now, four years later, he still becomes overjoyed at the sight of that target stick.

Once your dog masters targeting, you can use the target to teach him many useful tricks. My dog learned to close kitchen cabinet doors, close bedroom doors, turn lights on and off, and wipe his feet. He has even learned to close the toilet lid. He closes the lid instead of drinking from the toilet.

You can buy training target sticks (see Resources, page 194) or you can even use a tree branch. I found that an old radio antenna is great because you can telescope it to different lengths. A telescoping stick comes in handy later when you begin *fading the cue* (page 183).

Hold the stick out for your dog to look at. When he comes over and touches it with his nose, click and treat. If he doesn't touch it, but looks at it, click and treat. If he's not interested, rub a little peanut butter or cheese on the tip of the stick. When he smells it or licks it, click and treat.

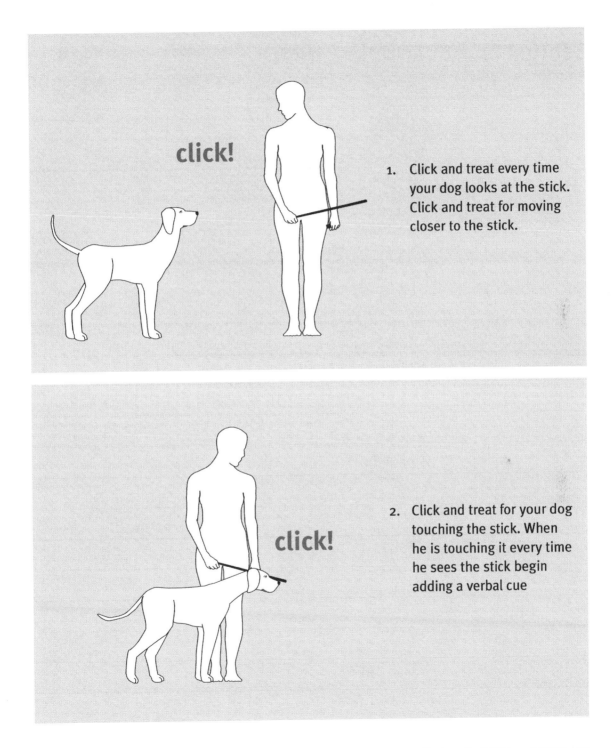

click!

1. Click and treat every time your dog looks at the stick. Click and treat for moving closer to the stick.

click!

2. Click and treat for your dog touching the stick. When he is touching it every time he sees the stick begin adding a verbal cue

Target Stick/Targeting: (Part 2)

After your dog is coming over and touching the stick every time he sees it, you can begin adding a ***verbal cue*** (see page 182). I use three verbal cues for this game. I teach only one cue at a time. "Nose" for touching it with his nose, "Paw" for touching it with his paw, and "Touch" if I don't care how he touches it.

Once you have added the cue, don't click and treat him for touching the stick unless you have given the cue. Make a game of it. Hold out the stick, but don't say the cue. If he touches it, ignore him. Then show it to him again, but this time, give the cue. Click and treat him if he touches it.

Make sure to play this game in many different locations. Have your dog learn to follow the stick. Pretend his nose is drawn to it like a magnet. Move it up high, low, and under things for a click and treat.

Some dogs bite at the stick. Initially click and treat him for any contact with the stick. After he seems to understand the game, begin clicking for only touching the stick without biting. A bite on the stick gets nothing. A gentle touch on the tip of the stick will earn a click and treat.

After your dog knows a cue for this trick, you can begin making it useful. You can begin transferring the touch to other objects such as doors, light switches, or specific toys (see Nose, page 100, or Paw, page 104).

Many animal trainers use other objects such as their own hands as targets. Experiment and see which target works best for you and your dog.

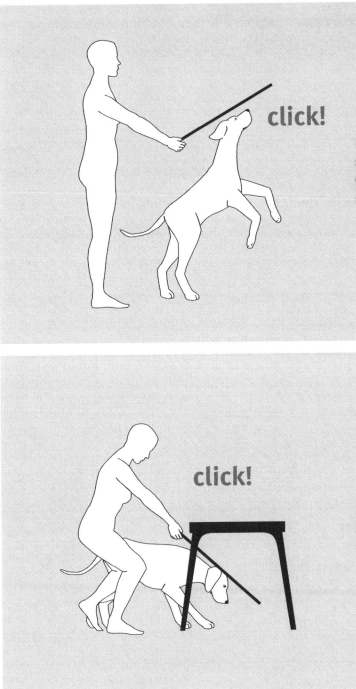

click!

Hold the stick in progressively harder positions. Click and treat for every successful touch.

click!

Be creative and find ways to challenge your dog

Nose

Many dogs you see performing in the movies or on television are simply doing a variation of the "Nose" trick. This basic trick is the foundation for other useful tricks. For example, my dog has learned how to close doors. I find this really useful when I'm working at my computer. If he barges in, I simply send him back to close the door without stopping my work.

An excellent use for the "Nose" trick is to teach your dog to target your hand. You can then ask your dog to touch your hand to distract him from barking at another dog or acting too friendly with a visitor. Touching your hand also puts him at your side walking nicely on his leash.

Teach your dog to transfer his "Nose" touch from the target stick (see page 96) to a new object. Move your target stick to the object that you want him to touch with his nose. When he touches both objects, click and treat. After he touches both objects several times, begin clicking and treating only when he touches the new object. Then gradually begin moving the target stick farther away from the new object.

To teach your dog to close cabinet doors with his nose, teach him to touch a piece of paper with the target stick. Click and treat every time he touches both the target stick and the paper with his nose. Then tape the paper on the open door. Tell him to "Nose." When he is confidently touching the paper, begin moving the target stick farther away from the paper. When he touches the paper every time he hears the cue, cut down the size of the paper.

(Continued, next page)

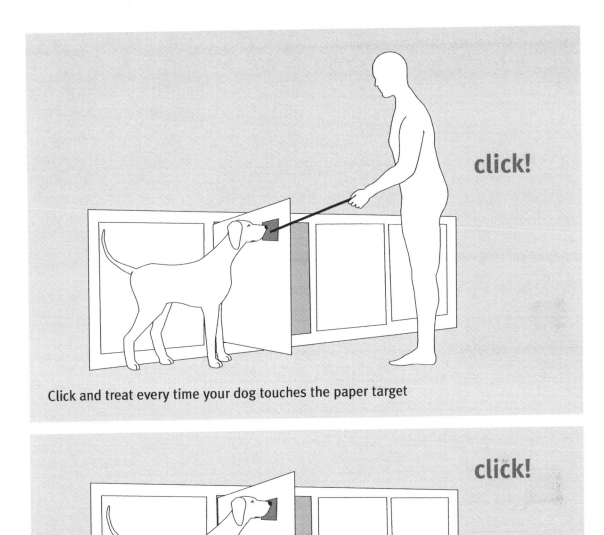

click!

Click and treat every time your dog touches the paper target

click!

Begin moving the target stick away from the paper target. Click and treat when he touches only the paper target.

Continue to reduce the size of the paper until it's gone. Then begin clicking only for harder pushes. Finally begin clicking only for pushes that completely close the cabinet. Once you teach this trick, and someone leaves a cabinet open, your dog can come up and slam it closed. My dog is now teaching my husband how to close cabinet doors.

Note: The signal or cue for my dog to close a cabinet door is simply an open cabinet door. I enjoy having him close the door every time it is left open. I click and give him a treat every time he closes a cabinet, even when I have not given him a *verbal cue* or *signal* (pages 182-183).

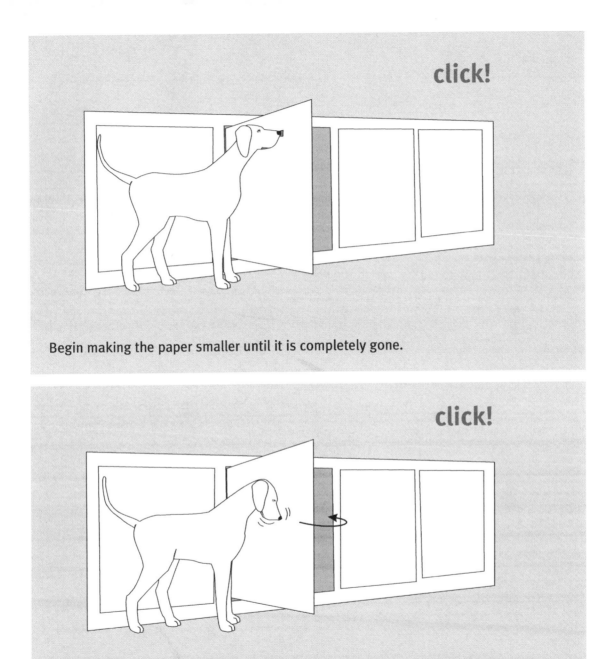

click!

Begin making the paper smaller until it is completely gone.

click!

When he is touching the open door, begin clicking and treating for only pushes that move the door. Finally, click only for pushes that close the door completely.

Paw

Uses

Turning off lights

Waving

Giving a High Five

This is another basic skill that is the foundation for other useful tricks.

Many people prefer their dogs to use their nose instead of using their paws, because they are concerned about dogs scratching objects with their nails. I don't find it a problem because I keep my dog's nails trimmed short. I use a small cordless electric nail grinder to keep them smooth.

You teach "Paw" the same way as you teach "Nose." For example, to teach your dog to turn off lights, put your target (see page 96) on the switch. Give your cue for him to touch the target with his paw. Click and treat. After he begins touching the switch regularly, gradually eliminate the target stick. Next, begin clicking only when he moves the switch. After he is beginning to move the switch, you can change the cue from "Paw" to another cue like "Light" or "Switch." Dana Babb, owner of Paws Abilities in Seattle, teaches service dogs who help people that have disabilities. She suggests that you teach your dog to push the switch up with his nose and paw it down with his paw.

Now sit back and ask your dog to turn out the lights.

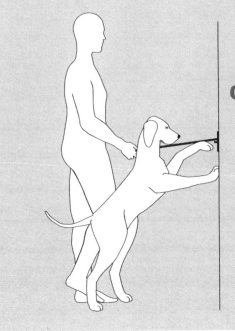

click!

Use a target stick to teach your dog to touch the light switch

click!

Gradually fade the target stick and click and treat your dog for pawing the switch.

Next, click for the times that he turns off the switch.

Spin

Uses

Wiping muddy paws

Stretching muscles

Showing children a trick

Having fun

I love this trick. It's a perfect example of what looks like a silly trick, but is really very useful. I live where it rains all year-round, and I have very light-colored carpets (I now know better). I have the dream dog who wipes his feet before coming in the house. I ask him to spin on the doormat. Another use many dog owners have found for the spin is to warm up their dog's muscles. This helps prevent injuries to dogs participating in competition events.

One way to teach this trick is to use the target stick (see page 96). Begin by teaching your dog to touch the stick with his nose. Once he will follow the stick, start moving it so that he needs to turn his head to touch it. Click and treat. Gradually move the stick so he must turn his body. Don't expect a complete circle at first. Click and treat for portions of a circle. Gradually work up to a full circle, then to two circles. When your dog can spin around several times, begin fading the target stick. I do this by shortening the stick in some way. You can cut it off, or slide it up your arm. Continue until the stick has disappeared and you can just move your finger in a circle as a *signal* (page 183).

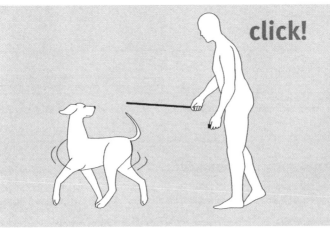

click!

Click and treat for your dog
following the target stick in
a partial circle.

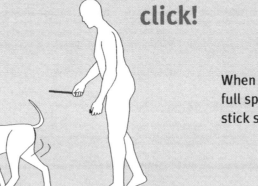

click!

When he completes several
full spins, start making the
stick shorter.

click!

Continue making the stick
shorter until it disappears.
Use your finger as a signal
for a spin.

Toss

Uses

Teach dogs self control

Teaches the verbal cue "Wait" or "Leave it"

Teach dogs coordination

Fun

At the 1999 Association of Pet Dog Trainers (APDT) conference Donna Duford suggested the toss trick as a good way for dogs to learn self-control (great for puppies). This trick teaches dogs how to "Leave it" or "Wait." Your dog must learn to wait for a release word before flipping a cookie and eating it.

To teach the toss, begin by gently holding your dog's muzzle in your hand. Don't restrain him, just steady his nose. Quickly place a large cookie or object on his nose. Depending on the structure of your dog's face, you may have to place the object on top of his head or between his eyes. Experiment with your dog to find the best place for the cookie. Let go of the cookie and then let go of his nose. Let him snatch the cookie. Initially let him get the cookie with almost no waiting. Then while placing the cookie give him a **verbal cue** (page 182) like "Wait" or "Leave it." Very gradually increase the length of time that the object balances on his face. As you increase the time, begin to give a **release word** (page 186), so he knows when to flip and grab the treat. If you use a clicker, the click will become a release for the dog to grab the treat. Don't expect a puppy to hold still for very long with a cookie on his nose. Remember to increase the difficulty very slowly so that he has plenty of success.

If your dog tries to grab the cookie while you're putting it on his nose, put the treat down or hold it behind your back without saying anything. Only continue when your dog holds still and waits while you place the cookie.

(Continued, next page)

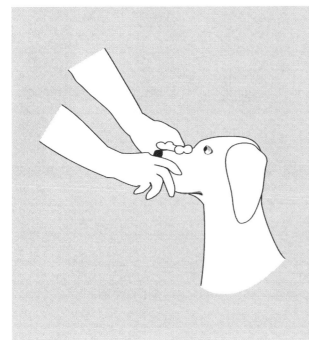

Place a cookie on your dog's face while gently holding his nose. Let go of the cookie first and then immediately release his nose.

Extend the time (in very small steps) that you have him "Wait."

My dog saw no sense in flipping the cookie into the air. He just waited for the release word, then he lowered his nose and let the cookie drop to the floor. I was about to give up when I tried placing one of his toys between his eyes. He flipped it into the air. Now he loves to play this game with a variety of toys. After many months of flipping his toys, he learned to flip a cookie. So experiment to get the results you want. Every dog will do this trick differently.

Caution: This is not a trick that children should teach. The dog may be so quick at snatching the treat that children cannot get their hands out of the way. Your dog could accidentally bump or scratch a hand. Legally this bump or scratch could be considered a dog bite.

Give your release word.

Put It Away

This is a very useful trick. It really impresses people, but more importantly it gives your dog a real job. Once he learns, maybe your dog can then teach the kids how to put things away.

To start teaching this trick, your dog must know how to give you objects (see page 68).

1. Begin this trick by teaching your dog to drop an object into a container. Put a basket or toy box on the floor right under his head. Hand your dog the object, hold your hand over the box, and immediately cue him to "Give" the object. Don't take the object. Instead let it drop into the box with a thud. Click as he drops the object into the container. Give him a treat.

2. Begin by moving your dog a step away from the box before handing him the object. This makes him take a step to the box before dropping the object. After a few drops, stop saying the word "Give," but be sure to click and treat every time he drops the object in the box. When he clearly understands that you want him to drop it in the box, begin saying a new cue like "Put it away" or "Clean up."

3. Start moving farther away from the container. Hand your dog the object. Have him move to the box to drop it. If he does, click and treat. If he doesn't drop it in the box, then decrease the distance to the box. Continue until you can move several feet away from the box. Give him the cue and click and treat him when he takes the object from you and puts it in the box. Only click for drops that land in the box.

(Continued next page)

(Continued next page)

Uses

Putting away toys

Putting away laundry

Picking up and putting away dropped objects

Putting dog dishes in the dishwasher

Serving as a good example for other family members

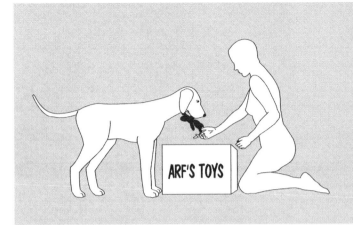

1. Hand your dog a toy. Have him drop it in your hand. Let it fall from your hand to the box. Gradually lower your hand so the toy is dropping in the box. Click and treat.

2. Continue handing the toy to him, but increase the distance he must move to drop it in the box. Click and treat successful drops into the box.

3. Begin sitting farther from the box. Click and treat when he begins taking the toy to the box without you.

4. The next step is to teach your dog to pick up the object off the floor. Start by moving close to the box. Make sure your dog has success as you make the task a little harder. Put the object on the floor next to the box. Click and treat when he takes the object and drops it in the box. When he begins consistently putting the object the box, begin moving it farther away from the box.

5. In very small, incremental steps begin moving away from the box and your dog.

Every dog is different. Don't be afraid to experiment; you and your dog are both learning. Both of you are going to make mistakes, but that's all part of learning. With clicker training, mistakes don't hurt.

Have fun and impress your family and friends with your canine house-cleaner service.

4. Put the toy on the floor. Click and treat him for dropping it in your hand (or in the box). Be sure to move back to holding your hand over the box.

5. Begin gradually moving away from the box again. Click and treat when your dog picks up a toy and puts it in the box.

6. Now have your dog teach the rest of the family.

Trick Suggestions: Some Useful/Some Silly

A creative group of clicker enthusiasts compiled this list of tricks on an Internet clicker E-mail list.

Impressive Tricks

- Bare teeth ("Be a wolf" or "What do sharks look like?") I don't suggest this if you have a big, menacing-looking dog.
- Bark (speak)
- Bark silently (Whisper/speak softly)
- Bark LOUD (shout)
- Beg (dog sits up and holds up paws)
- Bite water or snap at air (away from anyone's face!)
- Bow
- Circle me
- Tilt your head to one side
- Crawl
- Did you wash your hands? (dog sits up in Beg position but shows pads)
- Dig
- Fan the flames (two paws)
- Figure 8 (walk in a figure 8)
- Growl
- High four ('high five,' but for a dog!)
- Kiss
- Nod your head
- Nose touch to hand
- Nose touch to other objects (naming objects or just pointing)
- Play dead
- Paw touch to objects
- Push things with paw (like doors, drawers)
- Put paws on a person's shoulders
- Ring bell by pulling string
- Ring bell with nose
- Ring bell with paw
- Roll over
- Rub muzzle on floor
- Shake hands
- Shake your head
- Shake yourself
- Sit on couch with front feet on ground
- Spin
- Wag tail
- Walk backwards
- Wave
- Wave/shake hands with the other paw
- Where's your tail?
- Whimper
- Yawn

Amazing Tricks

- Balance treat on nose, then toss it up in the air and catch it
- Carry purse or other bag
- Cover your eyes
- Fetch newspaper
- Fetch slippers
- Find and bring dog dishes
- Find and bring keys
- Find and bring leash
- Find and bring TV remote
- Get a toy by name
- Heel backward
- Hide your eyes
- Hide your head (nose under cushion or blanket)
- Howl
- Lead another dog by the leash (or lead himself by the leash)
- Limp
- Moonwalk (scoot backwards in a bow)

- Wear sunglasses or hat
- Pick a card (from a deck)
- Pick the hammer (use paw to show correct tool)
- Pull on harness: pulling kids on sled, pulling Christmas tree home from lot, pulling laundry basket, pulling firewood, pulling cart
- Pull on rope: close doors, open doors, open cupboards, pull wheelchairs
- Pull your wallet out of your pocket
- Push balls with nose
- Push something with the nose
- Put toys away
- Ride a cart
- Ride a skateboard
- Roll to the left/roll to the right
- Rub back on floor
- Rub muzzle with paws
- Sit in a chair, paws on table
- Sneeze
- Take a bow, twirl, and take a bow.
- Take money from someone else and bring it to you!
- Walk sideways
- Weave between your legs

- Climb a ladder
- Dance
- Kick balls with paws (soccer)
- Learn names of family members and carry messages back and forth
- Nose or paw touch to designated colors or shapes
- Roll over with ball between front paws
- Stop on cue
- Walk up stairs backward

Unbelievably impressive tricks

- Fetch soda from fridge
- Bang! (roll over on side and look dead, except tail, usually)
- Bring you a Kleenex when you sneeze
- Carry basket with Halloween treats to door (wearing costume). Open door and hide behind it, dog walks forward to doorsill and sits politely while children take treats.
- Count/Add/Subtract (What's one and three? What's 312 minus 308? the cue is a tiny hand signal to bark)

- Learn sentences: Show me your dish, Show me the dog food, Show me where water comes from
- Lie on blanket, grab one corner of blanket, roll over and cover yourself up and pretend to sleep
- Pick up everything that's on the floor and put it in garbage
- Say your prayers (Beg position, front paws on chair, nose tucked in between front legs)
- Steal people's purses from beside chairs and put them in a bucket
- Stop, Drop and Roll (for showing fire safety to kids)

Contributors:
James Leatherwood
Jean Heisler
Chris Nielsen
Kim Burrell
Susan Finlay Ailsby
Kay Laurence
Stacy Braslau-Schneck
Stephanie Price

Chapter 6
Super Clicking

Becoming a Super Clicker

This section supplies activities and information to help you refine your teaching. When you and your dog are ready to learn more, use the following pages to help you and your dog do skills faster, more reliably, and in any location. This section also explains how you can eliminate the clicker. There are charts to help you keep track of your teaching progress. I have also included information on how to find a non-coercive dog training class.

On page 121 are Karen Pryor's 1996 *Fifteen Rules of Shaping* derived from her book, *Don't Shoot the Dog*. These rules have spread worldwide due to the Internet and Karen's seminars. They are an excellent review of the complete clicker training process.

Karen Pryor's *Fifteen Rules of Shaping*

1. Raise criteria in small enough increments so that the subject always has at least 50% chance of getting reinforced on any particular try.

2. Raise one criterion at a time: first height, then speed. Or first speed, then height. Don't try to establish two new criteria with the same click.

3. When you introduce a new criterion—when you're shaping a new aspect of the behavior—relax all the old standards temporarily.

4. Always put the current level of response on an intermittent schedule before raising criteria.

5. When the behavior is satisfactory, build it into the repertoire, and reinforce it with cues for other behavior.

6. When you are not using the behavior in a chain or in the repertoire, go to a variable schedule, only reinforcing an occasional response.

7. When you are shaping a behavior involving time (a long down) or distance (tracking) bounce back and forth between harder and easier tasks; keep the animal hopeful and guessing.

8. If one shaping procedure is not making progress, find another path up the mountain; there are as many ways to get behavior as there are trainers to think them up.

9. Don't interrupt a training session gratuitously; that constitutes a punishment.

10. If behavior deteriorates, 'go back to kindergarten': quickly review the whole shaping procedure with a series of earned reinforcements. Back up and do an easy review, also, when asking for new behavior in difficult circumstances or a new environment.

11. Keep your training sessions short and frequent; three five-minutes sessions will get you further, faster, than one hour-long session. Fit the occasional cue, click, and treat into the daily routine, wherever you can.

12. Change pace frequently during a session: reinforce new, demanding work (precision heeling, say) with easy, fun work (tricks, jumping.)

13. When an animal is volunteering a behavior over and over, that's the time to start teaching a cue for that behavior; don't introduce a cue until the behavior exists.

14. Don't try to correct mistakes with punishment or leashpops, let the subject LEARN from its own experience which behaviors get reinforced (clicked) and which don't. Learning goes faster without aversives.

15. Quit while you're ahead. If you run into difficulties with a particular behavior, or pass the point of fatigue, postpone that task to another session, and ask for something easier; try to end each session on a high note.

Karen Pryor, May 1996

Take it on the Road

Uses

Helping your dog understand how to get a click

Teaching your dog that the game works in many locations

Creating reliable skills

While teaching, change your position often. Don't always sit or always stand. Change rooms or go outside. Otherwise dogs believe that they should do the skill only in the room or position that they first learned it.

Have your dog learn to do each skill in many different environments. Gradually introduce things that distract your dog. Start by asking him to do the things he knows best while out in public. Don't be discouraged if he seems to forget. Be ready to go ***Back to Kindergarten*** (see page 187) which means going back as many steps as necessary for your dog to be successful. Gradually increase the difficulty of the skill. For example, if you're teaching a stay, gradually increase the time your dog must stay. Then begin adding more difficult distractions. Click and treat just the way you taught the skill the first time. The more places and distractions you introduce, the more reliable his behavior will be.

Ask for the skill in progressively more difficult places.

Be sure to ask for the skill only if you think your dog will be successful.

Fading the Clicker

Replacing the clicker with a verbal marker

The purpose of the clicker is to tell your dog what he is doing right. It is a marker that promises he will get a treat. When you're first teaching a new game, it's very important that you mark the exact second your dog does the action. After he understands what you want, he does not need the exactness of the clicker. You can then start replacing the clicker with a word or verbal marker (page 188) like "Yesssss" or whatever word or noise you want.

To replace the clicker, begin by saying your ***verbal marker*** just before you click. Then gradually stop using the clicker, but continue saying your verbal marker. Always give a treat when using a verbal marker, just as you did with the clicker.

Don't toss your clicker away. You'll want to use it to teach new things to your dog. It is your way of communicating with him. Think of it as dog language and use it often. Many clicker trainers occasionally use the clicker as a refresher.

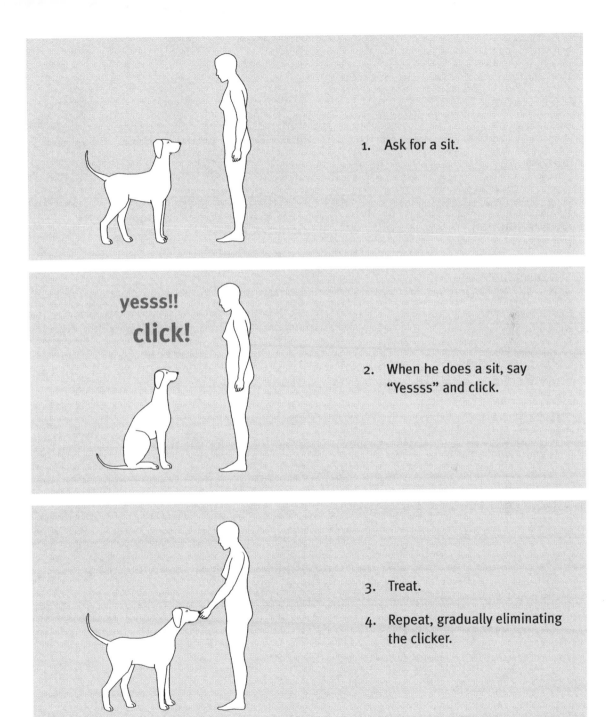

1. Ask for a sit.

yesss!!
click!

2. When he does a sit, say
   "Yessss" and click.

3. Treat.

4. Repeat, gradually eliminating
   the clicker.

Vary the Treat

Uses

Keeping your dog excited and interested

Making sure that your dog doesn't get bored with one kind of treat

Helping you continue learning what is most reinforcing to your dog

While you can eliminate the clicker, it's important that you always give a reward for a job well done. It doesn't have to be a food treat. It can be play or whatever is a reward for your dog. Change the rewards often and surprise your dog.

I make a mixture of treats and put them in a bowl. Then I grab a treat out of the bowl without looking. Sometimes it is one of my dog's favorites. Sometimes it isn't. This keeps him guessing and he never knows when he will get a really great treat.

He gets a *jackpot* (see page 184) when he makes a big leap in learning. I also give him very special treats when he does something that is very difficult, like coming away from a cat when I call.

Play may also be a reward for your dog. You can mix treats and play. Test your dog to see if play is a good reinforcement for him. After you click and play with him, does he repeat the skill you were working on? If he does, then a mixture of play and treats may be reinforcing to your dog.

Here are some suggestions for varying the treats.

1. Use a variety of treats in each session.
2. Use high-value treats (whatever he is crazy about) in distracting environments.
3. Use his favorite toys. Use them only while training. Put them away after the teaching session.
4. Use your dog's natural talents as treats: retrieving, sheep herding, sled pulling, and hunting.

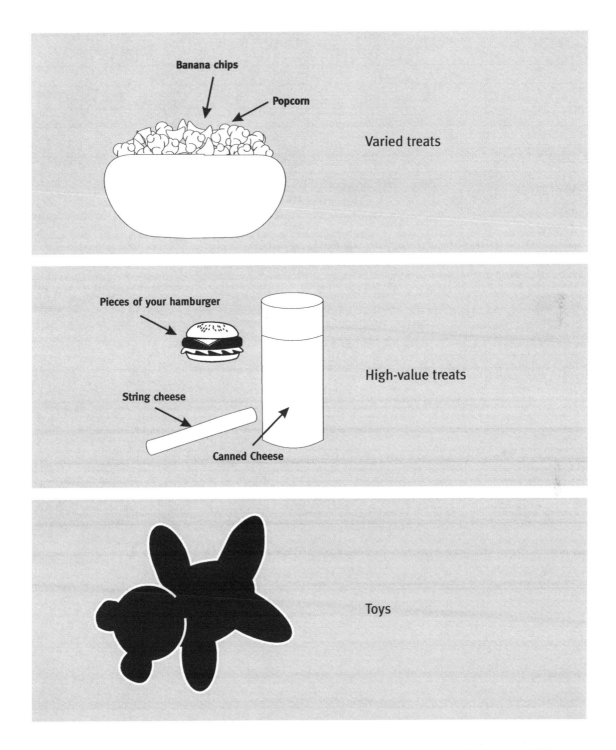

Banana chips

Popcorn

Varied treats

Pieces of your hamburger

String cheese

Canned Cheese

High-value treats

Toys

Teaching Charts

Keeping track of your teaching successes

Many people like the idea of keeping track of their dog's progress. This is a good idea if you're teaching several different games or skills. On pages 131-132 is a chart for you to keep track of your progress. Make a copy of the chart for each activity you are teaching your dog.

On page 129 is an example of how to fill out the chart.

1. Write your goal in the first block. Be as detailed as you can. This will help with the next step.
2. Break the skills down into small steps and list them.
3. When your dog completes a step, give yourself and your dog a star and write down the session number. In my example, Arf turned his head and his upper body to the left in the first session. Ann gave him a star for steps one and two, and wrote down the session number, 1. If after a few minutes, your dog has not completed a step, go back to the previous step where he was successful (see ***Going Back to Kindergarten***, page 187).
4. After your dog successfully has completed all the steps you listed, begin adding your ***verbal cue or signal*** (see pages 182).
5. After you have the skill on a cue, make sure your dog successfully accomplishes the skill in many different places. If he doesn't remember a skill in a new location simply go back to your list of steps (2) and review them with a few clicks.
6. When your dog will do the skill wherever you ask, then you can gradually eliminate the clicker. However, keep giving him treats, pats and praise.

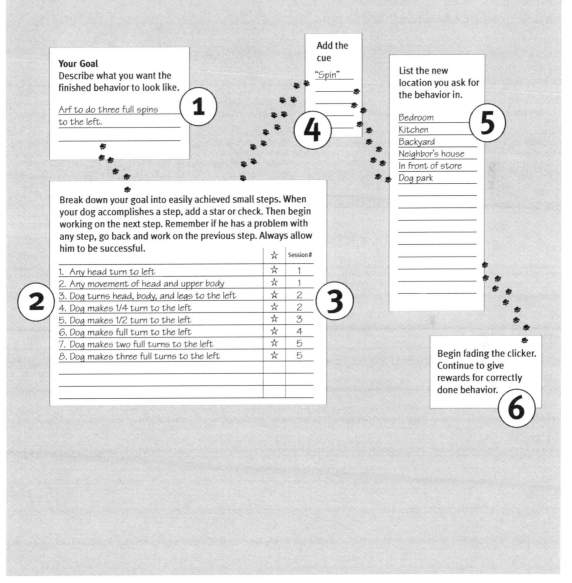

Your Goal
Describe what you want the
finished behavior to look like.

Arf to do three full spins
to the left.

1

Break down your goal into easily achieved small steps. When
your dog accomplishes a step, add a star or check. Then begin
working on the next step. Remember if he has a problem with
any step, go back and work on the previous step. Always allow
him to be successful.

	☆	Session #
1. Any head turn to left	☆	1
2. Any movement of head and upper body	☆	1
3. Dog turns head, body, and legs to the left	☆	2
4. Dog makes 1/4 turn to the left	☆	2
5. Dog makes 1/2 turn to the left	☆	3
6. Dog makes full turn to the left	☆	4
7. Dog makes two full turns to the left	☆	5
8. Dog makes three full turns to the left	☆	5

2

3

**Add the
cue**

"Spin"

4

**List the new
location you ask for
the behavior in.**

Bedroom
Kitchen
Backyard
Neighbor's house
In front of store
Dog park

5

Begin fading the clicker.
Continue to give
rewards for correctly
done behavior.

6

Your Goal
Describe what you want the finished behavior to look like.

_____

_____

_____

Break down your goal into easily achieved small steps. When your dog accomplishes a step, add a star or check. Then begin working on the next step. Remember if he has a problem with any step, go back and work on the previous step. Always allow him to be successful.

	☆	Session #

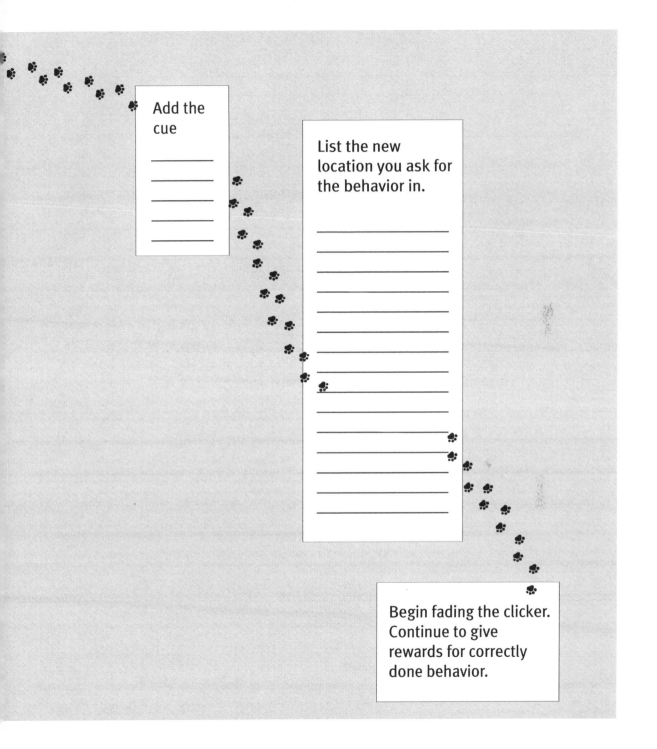

Add the cue

_____
_____
_____
_____
_____

List the new location you ask for the behavior in.

_____
_____
_____
_____
_____
_____
_____
_____
_____
_____
_____
_____
_____
_____

Begin fading the clicker. Continue to give rewards for correctly done behavior.

Finding a Class

Uses

Finding a class that uses positive teaching methods

Okay, so you've started training your dog and you think that taking a class would be fun. It will take a little work on your part to make sure that the class you take meets your needs. There are many choices. You can take a basic dog manners course. You can take a class directed at passing the American Kennel Club Canine Good Citizen test (see pages 169 and 195). Or you can take classes to get your dog an obedience, flyball, agility, or tracking title. Classes should be fun for both you and your dog.

First, decide what you want to get from a class. Then begin your search to find an instructor and class that will fulfill your needs and fit you and your dog.

Unlike other training methods, clicker training is not about your winning, or becoming alpha or top dog. It's about you both winning. You win by having a well-mannered canine friend. Your dog wins by understanding what makes you happy and by getting a reward. You both gain a great deal from the training process. You learn to communicate and bond with your dog. Your dog learns that he can control the consequences of his actions. You are not your dog's boss; you are his guardian.

If you bought this book and read this far you are probably interested in taking a clicker class. While clicker training is becoming very popular, not all areas of the world have *qualified clicker instructors* (see page 185). This should not stop you from joining a class. Simply get permission from the instructor to use a clicker in class. Don't make it a big deal, just click and treat as needed. You will, however, want to find a class that uses non-coercive methods (for both you and your dog). Not all classes are taught that way. Many classes advertise that they are gentle, humane, and use positive reinforcement. However, some of these instructors believe that you must use 'corrections' first and then follow with praise or a reward. This is not the way I believe dogs (or people) learn best. If you don't want to 'correct' your dog while he's trying to learn, I suggest you look for a class using the positive reinforcement part of operant conditioning (see page 185).

If you have permission to click in a non-clicker class, it's important for the instructor to tell you what they will teach at the next class. This will allow you to introduce your dog to the new skill in a gradual, positive way. Use the class to practice and refine the skill in a distracting location. If your dog doesn't know the skill the class is working on, then work on a skill your dog knows. Train the new skill in small incremental steps at home.

To help you find a class, I have included forms (pages 134-137) for you to copy and fill out for a class you are interested in taking. The first one is for the phone interview you should conduct. The second one is for you to fill out while observing a class (before you sign up). Be sure you interview and observe the person that will actually be teaching your class.

Copy these pages and fill out one for each class you are interested in taking.

**Two roads diverged in a wood, and I—
took the one less traveled by,
And that has made all the difference.**

—Robert Frost

Phone Interview Form

Class Name_____ Phone_____

Start Date_____ Time_____ Cost_____

Your Questions

What are the qualifications of the person that will teach the class? See page 185 for information on qualifications of instructors.

Do they require a choke, a check, or slip collar? These are for correcting a dog. They are used in correction-based training classes. Avoid these classes.

What are their teaching philosophies/learning theories?

Number of dogs in class? (Most clicker trainers find that beginning classes are best limited to eight dogs).

Can you observe the class (without your dog)? They should allow you to observe.

What books and videos do they recommend you read before the class? Read them and see if you agree with what they say.

Do they have assistants? What are their qualifications? Will they be helping with the actual instructing?

Are clickers allowed? Do they say yes, but then try to convince you don't need a clicker? Do they ask you what you want to get out of the class (socialization, an obedience title, or a specific solution to a problem)?

Do they encourage the entire family to come and work with your dog? Dog training affects everyone in the family. A dog is smart enough to learn from everyone in his family.

The Instructor's Answers

Class Observation Form

Class Name_____ **Phone**_____

Start Date_____ **Time**_____ **Cost**_____

What to Look for at a Class

Does the instructor tell the students to correct their dogs (using squirt bottles, leash pops, or loud commands)? Or do they show you how you can get the skill without corrections?

Does the instructor encourage the students to use a variety of reinforcements (food, toys, or play)?

Do the students ask questions? Are they answered?

Are all the dogs wearing the same kind of collar to correct their behavior? (This shows that the instructor is not helping students find individual solutions.)

Are all the students doing the same things simultaneously (drill)? Each dog and handler should be encouraged to learn at their own rate.

Is the instructor correcting the people, or kindly showing them a positive way to succeed? Do the dogs seem happy or are they nervous (licking, yawning, barking)?

Are the humans relaxed, smiling, and comfortable?

Does the instructor see dogs as adversarial? Do they explain a dog's action as sneaky, deceitful, or stubborn?

Does the instructor criticize other training methods, but doesn't explain why they don't work?

Your Observations

Chapter 7
Creating a Safe Dog

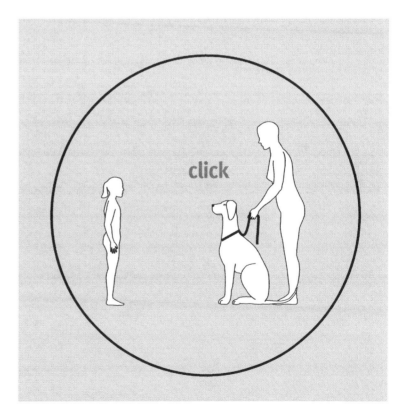

Preventing Chewing or Nipping

Uses

Avoiding scratches and nips

Stopping potentially dangerous behavior

We cannot speak dog language, so we must guess at why dogs chew on all kinds of objects and sometimes nip at hands and clothes. Although this may be annoying from a puppy, it can be serious in an adult dog. Here are two common reasons why dogs chew and nip.

Dogs Don't Have Hands

Your dog explores his environment with his mouth. A child can use his hands. Puppies and dogs grab with their teeth. Often dogs grab at you with their mouths to get your attention.

If your puppy nips or bites, startle him with a loud "Ouch." This is similar to what puppies do with each other. The loud "Ouch" doesn't work with all puppies. If he continues nipping, turn your back on him or leave the room. Any time the puppy stops nipping, click and give him a treat. Then be sure to play with him. Remember to reward what you want (gentle mouths) and ignore what you don't want (nipping and grabbing).

Use the clicker to teach the Doggie Zen game on page 60. This game will help to teach your puppy self-control. If the puppy or dog is chewing your things, teach the Leave It game on page 62.

He is Teething

When dogs are teething, chewing makes their gums feel better. Give him puppy-safe toys. I found that a product called Gumabone (see page 163) seems to work best for teething puppies. Another solution for a teething puppy is to give him ice cubes. Puppies love them and it does help sore gums.

Ouch!

If your dog nips, try saying "Ouch" loudly to startle him.

If he continues, turn your back or leave the room. Click and treat or begin playing with him when he stops nipping.

Solutions for Possession Guarding

Uses

Avoiding aggression problems

Avoiding law suits and possible loss of your dog

A dog is possession guarding when he guards his food, toys, you (or your family), or your property. This is a very serious problem. Signs of possession guarding are growling and not allowing anyone near him and his possession. A dog who is possession guarding may only act distressed at first, but often this behavior escalates into biting. If your dog is showing any signs of possession guarding, immediately see an *animal behaviorist* (see page 180). Make sure the behaviorist is qualified to handle your dog's problem. Get references and check credentials. Your dog's life, your safety, and your financial security may depend on you finding the right person.

The best way to avoid having a dog that guards possessions is training. Only adults should work on this prevention training. Don't do this prevention training if your dog is frightened or very nervous. Don't do this training with a dog you don't know.

Prevention of Food Guarding

Teach your dog that good things come from your hands. Clicker training helps teach this because we are always tossing or handing our dogs treats. You can also reinforce this training by teaching your dog to sit and wait until you put down his food bowl. Click or give your release word, then back off several steps and allow your dog to eat. Don't disturb or lean over him. If this does not distress him, then click and gently toss a really good treat into his bowl. Over several days (or weeks) gradually move closer till you can put the treat in the bowl with your hand. Don't annoy or tease him. The final stage of this process is to be able to remove his bowl while he is eating. Add a special treat and give the bowl right back to him. This prevention program is best done with a puppy less than three months old. If you feel any of these stages distress your dog, don't continue and please consult an animal behaviorist.

Prevention of Toy Guarding

Teach your dog the Leave It Game (page 62) or Give Game (page 68). Routinely take the toy and give it back. If you see any signs of aggression or you are unable to take the object from your dog, consult an animal behaviorist.

Prevention of People Guarding

The prevention for this problem is to socialize your dog (see Socialization, page 156). Consult an animal behaviorist if you see any signs of unfriendliness to people while doing the socialization program. One of the most important signs of a developing problem is fear. Most dog bites are from 'fear biters.' People often unintentionally teach dogs to fear things. If your dog is frightened of something new don't try to reassure him. Don't say things like "That's okay." Don't reinforce his fears. Instead, reinforce his bravery and ignore his silly fears.

Also, it is a good idea to have your dog checked by a veterinarian. It is possible that your dog is fearful because he has a medical problem and is in pain.

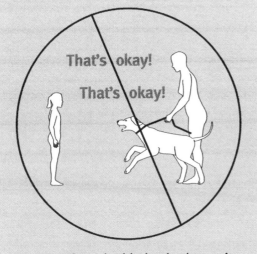

Don't reinforce bad behavior by saying "That's okay."

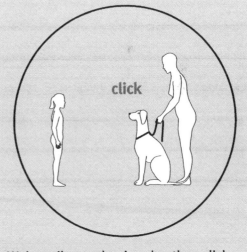

Wait until your dog is calm, then click and treat him for good actions.

Children and Canine Safety

Uses

Teaching children how to behave around all dogs

I moved frequently as a child and often my only friend was my dog. Dogs can be very special friends to children; however, children must be taught to respect dogs. Teaching your child how to act properly around all dogs is extremely important. Never allow a child to tease or play rough with any dog. Young children (younger than five years old) should not be left alone with any dog. A knowledgeable adult should watch older children to decide if the child can be left alone with an individual dog. Even if a child is very good with dogs, some dogs are very afraid of all children. These dogs may have had a bad experience, or may have never been around children.

Clicker training is an excellent way for children to play with dogs. An adult should click the dog and allow very young children give the dog the treat. The child should learn to toss the treat to the floor. This way the dog can't accidentally nip. Older children can team up with one child clicking and another child tossing the treat.

Terry Ryan, a world renowned dog trainer, developed the Prevent-A-Bite Program for the People-Pet Partnership at Washington State University's College of Veterinary Medicine. The chart on page 145 lists the main points from this program.[1] Read this chart to your children and discuss it with them.

[1] Reprinted with permission from *The Toolbox for Remodeling Your Problem Dog*, by Terry Ryan, 1998, Howell Book House.

Please Do	leave dogs alone while they are eating or chewing a toy. If you reach down and pet the dog it might surprise and worry her. Do you always feel like sharing your candy bar?
Please Do	leave the dog alone while she's sleeping. After playing hard all day, you like to relax awhile, too. The dog might be having a bad dream and think you are part of it.
Please Do	always ask permission from an adult before going up to anyone's dog, even if you know the dog. Ask Granny, if it is Granny's dog. Ask the parents, if you are visiting a friend. Dogs can't say "I don't want to play now," but grown-ups are pretty good at figuring out how dogs feel.
Please Do	approach the dog from the side, never from the back or straight in front. Extend your hand and show the dog your knuckles. Be sure the dog sees you. Have you ever jumped when a friend touched you and you weren't looking? It's just not polite.
Please Do	pet the side of the dog's head or under the chin. If the dog stretches forward to sniff or seems friendly, it's her way of saying, "How about a pat?" If the dog pulls back and acts afraid or acts angry, don't pet the dog. It's her way of saying, "I don't feel like a pat." You might be tempted to comfort her if she seems shy. Leave her alone; your attention may just worry her more.
Please Do	knock on the neighbors' door and ask for help if your ball accidentally gets into their yard. If no one is home, ask your parents to help. Don't go into a dog's yard without permission. The dog might worry, just as you might if someone walked into your living room without an invitation.
Please Do	keep walking past a dog in a parked car. Don't reach into a dog's car even if you know the dog. The dog may look as if she wants to be patted, but she might worry that you may take something. Do you always feel like sharing your things with others?
If you	encounter a dog that seems very angry, stand like a post. Posts don't run, they don't make any noise. They just stand still. Do the same as the post. The dog will likely sniff you and go away. If you look at the dog, move your hands, talk or run, the dog will take more interest in you and won't go away as soon.

Playing Safely with Dogs

Uses

Teaching dogs how to respect humans

Bonding with your dog

Many people love playing with their dogs. Playing helps us bond with our dog, and is healthy for both dogs and humans. The more you play with your dog, the more he will learn that you are one of the best things in the world. Games exercise your dog both mentally and physically. I love to watch dogs learn, so, for me, playing clicker games is fun for both my dog and myself. There are many things for dogs and humans to learn together. Some are organized sports (see page 169) and some are just individual tricks and games.

Here are some basic rules that everyone should follow when playing with dogs.

1. Don't roughhouse with your dog. This is true for all ages, but teaching this rule to children is especially important. Dogs need to learn that biting a human, even in play, is never allowed.
2. Play with dog-safe toys, not sticks or items that could injure you or your dog.
3. Don't allow young children to play unsupervised with your dog.
4. Don't allow young children to run away screaming from your dog.
5. Young children should never play tug games with a dog.
6. All people should be careful about playing tug games. Many dog trainers recommend never playing tug. I believe it depends on the dog. If you do decide to play tug with your dog, teach him the Give Game (page 68) first. You must be able to stop the game when you want to stop.

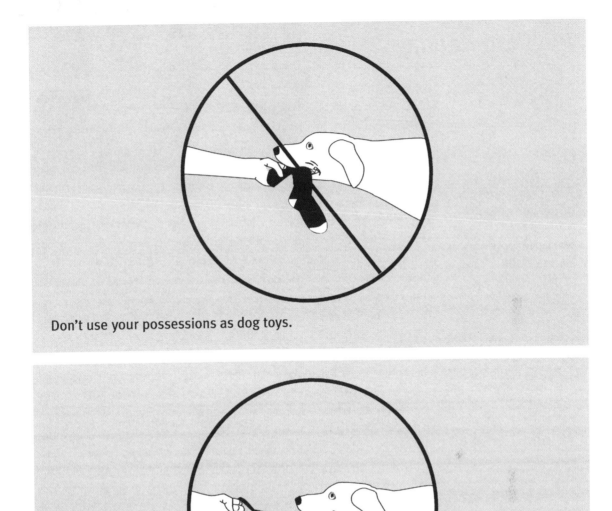

Don't use your possessions as dog toys.

Be sure to use a tug-toy with a handle long enough to keep your hands safe. Teach the Give Game (page 68) before playing the tug game.

Problem Barking

Uses

Avoiding neighbor-hood complaints

Keeping your house calmer

A dog who barks is not a danger to his owners. However, he is a danger to himself. One of the most common reasons dogs find themselves on death row at the animal shelter is uncontrolled barking. Neighbors often threaten owners with legal action if they can't stop their dogs from barking. You must teach your dog to be quiet. If your dog is barking when he is left alone, (see page 173).

Don't reward any kind of barking. This is the most important thing to remember when training your dog to stop barking. If you show your dog attention while he's barking at a cat walking past your house, he'll continue to bark. His reward might be as simple as the attention he gets from you yelling at him to be quiet.

Many clicker trainers have found that when a dog learns to bark on cue, he stops his barking. He learns to bark only when asked to "Talk" or "Speak." To teach this game, click and treat when he begins barking. He will stop to get his treat. Continue this game and put it on a ***verbal cue*** (see page 182). He learns that you reward him for barking only when you give the cue.

If your dog is 'demand barking' for you to do something like hurry up and get his dinner, simply quit. Freeze or put down his dog dish until he stops barking. When he does quit barking, pick it up the dish and continue. If he's barking in his crate to be let out, don't open the crate until he has stopped barking. Wait for thirty seconds (time it) of silence before letting him out.

Remember to ignore what you don't want and reward what you do want.

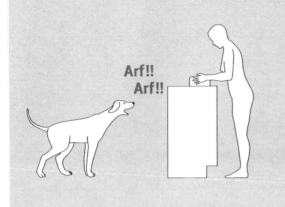

Your dog may 'demand' bark.
He's telling you to hurry up and
fix his food.

When this happens, stop.
Wait for thirty seconds of quiet.

After he is quiet for thirty seconds
begin fixing the food again. If he
starts barking again, stop again.

Chapter 8
A Dog's Bill of Rights

Your Responsibilities

Clicker training teaches with gentleness and fairness instead of with fear.

If you've chosen to bring a dog into your family, it's your responsibility to see that you meet all his needs. One of the most important of these is love. Clicker training helps build trust and affection between you and your dog. It helps you to learn how to communicate with him in a positive way. Clicker training shows you how to be gentle and fair instead of harsh and upset.

Dogs also need to be healthy. I don't discuss health requirements of dogs in this book; however, there are many wonderful books available. I suggest you investigate the wealth of knowledge on dog health.

Besides health care, dogs need nutritious food, safety, play, and companionship. The following pages offer suggestions on ways to give your dog what he needs in order to be a happy, cooperative canine friend.

Your Dog's Bill of Rights All dogs are entitled to, and deserve:

Healthy food

A secure environment

Stimulation

Socialization

Play

Peace and quiet

Companionship

A job

Understanding

Exercise

Healthy Food

Uses

Increasing your dog's energy

Improving overall health

Reducing veterinarian costs

Increasing your dog's lifespan

You need to learn what is nutritious and healthy for your dog. Start by understanding dog food labels. Your dog's age, activity level, and breed will determine what you should feed him. These factors will also determine how much and often to feed your dog. Wonderful books on canine diets are available from your library, Internet sites, or dog book catalogs like Dogwise (www.dogwise.com).

Determine how much to feed your dog by his weight and general condition. His eyes should be bright and his coat shining. According to Dog Breeder Florence Graham, owner of Graphic Standard Poodles in San Rafael, California, "You should be able to feel the structure of your dog under a nice covering of muscle and tissue. If you can't feel any structure at all, the dog is too fat. If your fingers get stuck between the ribs, he is too thin."

The best check for the effectiveness of a food is how the dog looks and acts. He should have large amounts of energy and his coat should be thick and shiny. Check for allergic reactions by looking inside your dog's ears. If they are very pink or red, he could have a food allergy.[1] Many people are feeding an alternative to commercial dog food. They are feeding fresh natural food. You can learn more about this approach on www.naturaldogfood.com.

Some of my students have shown concern about feeding training treats to their dogs. They fear that giving their dog a treat will encourage them to beg. Actually, clicker trained dogs rarely beg. They soon learn they must do something to earn a treat. Other people fear that their dog will become overweight. This will not happen if you give them the proper size and kind of treats. I use popcorn (without salt and butter) as a treat for my dog. Another favorite treat is small pieces of carrots. Check out the list of treats on page 11 and see what will work for your dog. If your dog is on a special diet, you can feed part of his daily ration (20%) as training treats.

[1] Dr. Pitcairn's Complete Guide to Natural Health for Dogs and Cats, Pitcairn, 1995.

Rice Flour, Beet Sug
Poultry Digest, Brewer's Dried Yea
, Brewer's Rice, Ethoxyquin, Poultry By-
assium Chloride, Meat Meal, Cellulose, Poultry
sodium Phosphate, Wheat Shorts, Iodized Salt, P
e Flour, Beet Sugar, Poultry Fat, Fish Meal, Ground C
st, Brewer's Dried Yeast, Meat-By-Products, Soy Flour,
ice, Ethoxyquin, Poul ct Meal, Potassium Cl
eat Meal, Cellulos t, Monosodium Phos
Wheat Shorts, I y-Product, Rice
Beet Su Fish Meal, Ground Corn
s Dried Yeast, Meat-By-Pro
r, Brewer's Rice, Ethoxyqui
y-Product Meal, Potassium
eat Meal, Cellulose, Poultr
odium Phosphate, Wheat
Salt, Poultry By-Produc
, Poultry Fat, Fish Me
, Brewer's Dried Ye
Rice, Ethoxyqui
Meat Meal

eat Shorts, Io
oultry By-Product,
eet Sugar, Poultry Fat
und Corn, Poultry Dige
Dried Yeast, Meat-By-
Flour, Brewer's Rice
y By-Product Me
t Meal, Cel

General Feeding Rules

- Read and understand dog food labels.

- Always provide fresh water.

- Feed adult dogs twice a day and puppies three to four times a day.

- Remove the food dish when your dog walks away.

- Wash dog food dishes after every feeding.

- Don't feed cooked bones. They may splinter.

- Don't feed table scraps. However, feeding balanced, fresh, whole food is okay.

- Provide an area for the dog to eat undisturbed by people or other pets.

- Don't let children near your dog while he is eating.

- Don't give dogs chocolate, sugar, or salt (many dog treats contain sugar and salt).

Socialization

**Helping to elimi-
nate aggression**

**Building confi-
dence**

Reducing fear

**Increasing your
enjoyment of your
dog**

**Expanding your
dog's freedom**

To have a well-adjusted dog, you need to introduce him to a variety of experiences. Well-socialized dogs are not fearful or aggressive, and understand how to behave safely.

The following chart will help you plan your socialization program. It's best if you can introduce your puppy to the things on this chart before he is five months old. However, if you haven't introduced your dog to these things as a puppy, don't give up. Slowly introduce your adult dog to the items on the chart. Click and treat your dog for moving closer to anything that worries him (see *Systematic Desensitization* on page 187). Don't baby him. Never tell him "That's okay" or "It's all right." You will only be rewarding him for being frightened of new places and things. Be careful not to exhaust your puppy or dog. Check with your veterinarian about when you can take your young puppy out in public.

Place a date or checkmark for each time you expose your dog to an item in the chart.

Babies (from a distance)										
Boy children (all ages)										
Girl children (all ages)										
Boy teenagers										
Girl teenagers										
Women adults										
Men adults										
Elderly women										
Elderly men										
People in wheel chairs										
People with walkers										
Hand-waving people										
Loud people										

Joggers									
People wearing hats									
People wearing glasses									
People wearing helmets									
People in unusual positions									
Pet shops									
Parking lots									
Parks									
New houses									
Schools (with permission)									
Kennels									
Grooming shop									
Parties									
Veterinarians									
Umbrellas									
Different floor surfaces									
City walks									
Country walks									
Car trips (to fun places)									
Bicycles									
Motorcycles									
Various vehicles									
Puppies									
Adult dogs									
Kittens									
Adult cats									
Horses									
Cows									
Other animals									

Companionship

Uses

Reducing stress

Reducing barking

Reducing damage

Creating a confident, happy dog

Dogs need companionship. Even if you have several dogs, they still need time with you. I strongly feel that we should allow all dogs to live in the house and to become part of the family. I feel that both dogs and people benefit from being together as much as possible.

People are often concerned by the destruction that dogs do while left alone. These dogs are not being vindictive or mean. They are often distressed at being left alone. Dogs are pack animals. Most wild canines never spend a minute of their lives alone. Even when wolves must leave their pups to go hunt, a nanny wolf stays with the pups. It's no wonder that our domestic dog often becomes stressed when his human pack leaves.

Your dog needs to learn that you will return. To teach him to trust that you come back, start by finding something to interest your dog (see pages 162-165) and leave for only two or three minutes at first. When you leave, tell him (in calm voice) "I'll be back," "Take care of things," or whatever words you wish to use. Just make sure you always say the same thing. Gradually increase the length of time that you stay away.

When you return, don't make a fuss over your dog or get him excited. Ask him to sit before you greet him. Don't feed him when you first get home; wait for a few minutes. Put away your groceries, sit and read the paper, or do anything that takes a few minutes. The idea is not to make a big deal out of your leaving and returning.

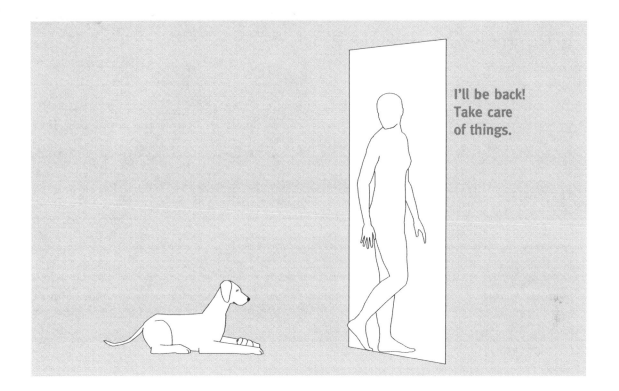

I'll be back!
Take care
of things.

Time left alone	List the time and date that you left your dog alone. First leave your dog for one minute. Repeat this first step five times before increasing the time to five minutes. Continue gradually increasing the time.				
1 minute					
5 minutes					
10 minutes					
30 minutes					
1 hour					
After an hour, increase the time you leave your dog in 1 to 2 hour increments.					

A Secure Environment

Uses

Keeping your dog safe and healthy

Keeping other animals and children away from your dog

Creating a safe training area

I recently received a phone call from one of my students who told me that a car had run over his sweet little puppy. The puppy died. The student was heartbroken. He was under the mistaken impression that his puppy would always stay at his side. Young puppies have a way of fooling us into thinking that they will always stay close to us. However, as puppies grow up, they begin to wander away and explore their world. When they become adolescent, they sometimes even forget their training temporarily. There is just no substitute for a secure environment if your dog is off his leash.

I want my dog to come when called 100% of the time. However, I know that I cannot bet his life on his understanding that he must come. Dogs hear and smell things that we aren't aware of. They don't understand dangers that we understand. They may become confused by our reactions, and panic. For these reasons I let my dog off the leash only when he is in a secure area.

Allowing dogs to run free is also illegal in many areas. Even in unpopulated areas, allowing your dog off the leash is often either illegal or unsafe. For example, parks (other than dog parks) often don't allow dogs to run free because dogs disturb the wildlife. In many areas dogs that chase domestic livestock may be destroyed. In farm country there is the possibility that your dog may find and eat poisons put out to control vermin. There are also natural dangers to your dog, including snakes, ticks, and burrs and barbed grass seeds.

If you live in an apartment or an area where you can't provide a fenced yard, I suggest you become involved in a dog activity or sports (page 169). These activities will give you a safe place to play and let your dog run.

Requirements for A Dog-Safe Yard	
Dig-resistant	Buried wire or concrete strip at base of fence
Jump-resistant	Extend the existing fence (see figure below)
Secure Gate	The latch should be dog- and child-proof
Toxin-free	Some plants, fertilizers, pesticides, fungicides, and paints can be toxic
Space	Large enough to teach and play with your dog

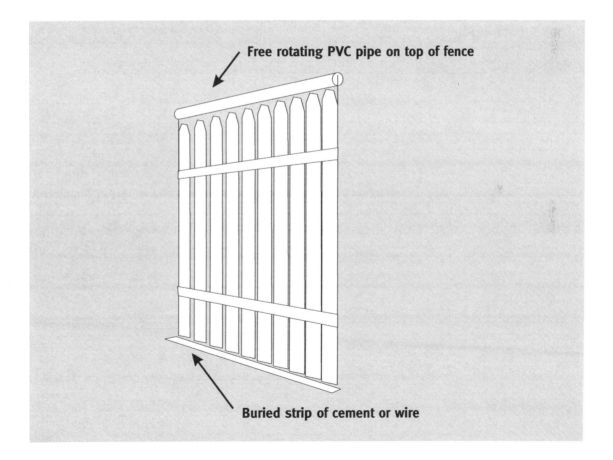

Free rotating PVC pipe on top of fence

Buried strip of cement or wire

Play

Uses

Providing physical exercise

Providing mental exercise

Training rewards

Having fun

All animals need to play. When we use positive reinforcement and the clicker, learning becomes play for both dogs and their humans. The clicker makes everything a game for dogs. Even practicing formal obedience heeling is a fun game for my dog.

However, dogs often need toys of their own to play with when we can't be with them. Fun toys are great clicker training rewards. Here are my suggestions on dog toys.

Nylabone and Gumabone Bones

These toys provide physical exercise and stimulation. The manufacturers claim that they are the longest-lasting chew toys made. I don't know if that is true or not, but I have one that is nineteen years old. It's still in great shape and ready for another generation. They're much cheaper than your dog chewing on your furniture or your shoes. I would purchase several because they come in different shapes and flavors. I also keep one in my car.

Kongs

I have a Kong that my dogs have chewed on for seventeen years. They do last. These are a necessity for all dogs. It helps chewers, 'home alone' dogs, and even barkers. The Kongs are hollow and come with instructions on how to stuff them with goodies to keep dogs from being bored. If you only get one toy, get this one.

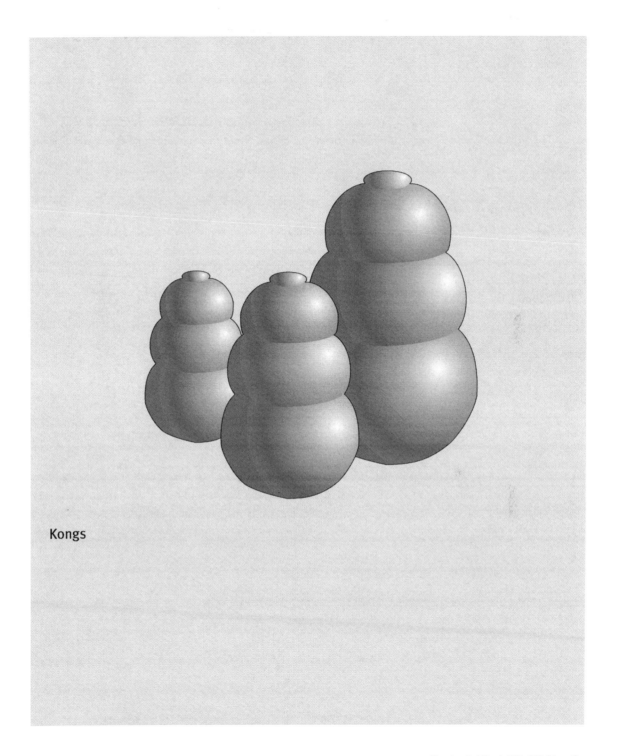

Kongs

Educational Toys

Some toys are so cleverly designed that they can be considered educational toys for dogs. These toys are teaching devices, not indulgences. They occupy active dogs and help them learn to think and solve problems.

Uses

Teaching dogs how to solve puzzles

Keeping dogs occupied

Buster Cube

This ingenious toy can help solve your dog's boredom problem. Your dog learns how to solve a puzzle. The toy is a hard plastic cube that holds dry food or treats. The treats only come out when a dog learns to roll the cube around. It comes with complete instructions to show you how to introduce your dog how to play with it. Buster Cubes come in two sizes. There are similar kinds of toys on the market that may be effective for your dog. Inspect any toy carefully for any parts that can break. Be sure to observe how your dog plays with the toy before leaving him alone with it.

Bully Ball

This is a very hard plastic ball known as a Bully Ball, or Best Ball. These balls are practically indestructible. They are excellent toys for 'home alone' dogs. Dogs can learn to play soccer with them or even to bowl. My dog loves to practice his herding with his ball. They come in a variety of sizes, even up to polar bear size.

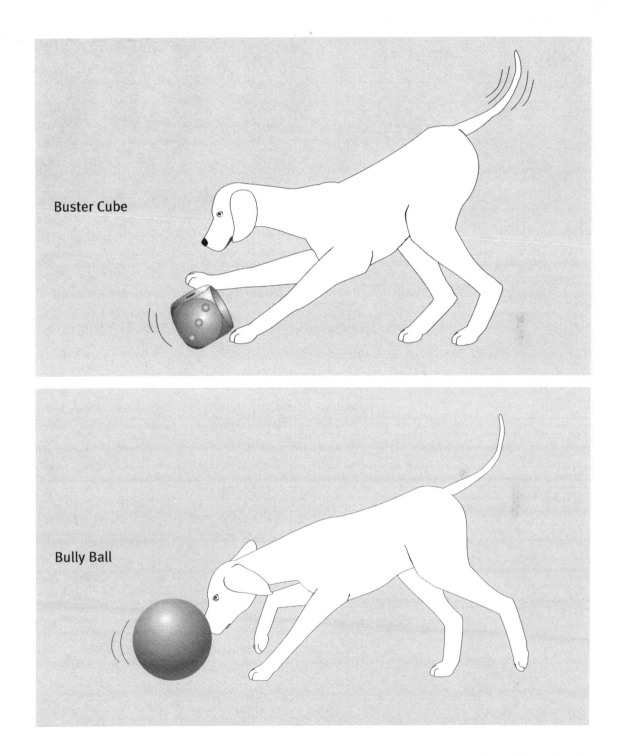

Buster Cube

Bully Ball

Jobs

Uses

Eliminating behavior problems

Keeping dogs healthy

Teaching dogs jobs

Most dog owners can't spend all day exercising and playing with their dogs. However, I believe that we can find ways to give our dogs both mental and physical exercise by giving them jobs to do. Giving them work or a job is great fun for them.

Most pet dogs don't have jobs to do, so they often invent a job. These clever dogs then go about their invented activity as if their lives depended on it. These activities might be digging up the back yard, or chasing every kid on the block. Punishment doesn't seem to stop them, but why should it? A wolf wouldn't last very long in the wild if a little pain stopped him from getting dinner. A border collie who is responsible for bringing back sheep from an area too steep for people wouldn't have any value if he gave up because the terrain was difficult.

Clicker training helps use your dog's determination. It gives him a job to do. It teaches him activities and makes him determined to make you click. Most of the activities in this book will help direct that determination. The clicker says "That is what I want." A good way to start getting your dog to work with you is to teach a game or a trick. Remember all the activities are just games to your dog, so pick something from this book and help him become a happy working partner.

While my dog is not a certified assistance dog, he knows many tasks that assistance dogs need to know. These activities are fun for him and he is a great help to me. He picks up articles that fall on the floor and gives them to me. He closes doors and turns on and off lights. So while I am working around my home, he is on duty and working right with me.

If your dog loves to grab items around the house, teach him to bring them to you, (see Get It Game, pages 72-75). You can even teach him to help you gather the laundry (page 112).

Teach your dog to pick up articles and bring them to you...

...or put them where they belong.

Exercise: Physical and Mental

Uses

Creating mental exercise

Creating physical exercise

Having fun for both you and your dog

Dogs love to learn, and they need physical exercise. To fill both needs, choose an activity that uses your dog's natural instincts. For example, if you have a herding breed, then you might like herding. You don't have to go out and buy the ultimate dog toy, a ranch. Instead, find someone that teaches herding, and take lessons. Your dog will love it.

Don't feel that you must limit yourself to what your dog was bred to do. Try any out any activities that you think might be fun, and see how your dog does.

The chart on the following pages lists many activities that you can learn to do with your dog. Dogs and their humans love these activities. Some people choose to do them just for fun and others find they love competition. It doesn't seem to matter to the dogs.

Use the clicker to help your dog learn these activities. For example, in the conformation show ring you can use the clicker to teach your dog proper foot, ear, and tail positions. Or, you can use the clicker to improve your dog's gait. In Agility, you can teach him to touch the contact zones. In competitive obedience training, you can click to tell him he's in the correct heel position. In flyball you can use the clicker to teach him how to use the flyball box.

Be aware of a dog's physical limitations. Don't ever ask a young dog (less than eighteen months) to jump higher then his elbows. If your dog is overweight or has joint problems, check with your vet about any jumping or playing on equipment.

To contact the organizations listed on the chart, see pages 195-198.

Dog-Related Activities

Activity	Description	Requirements	Organizations
Obedience	Dogs learn to do formal exercises with very specific rules. They can earn titles and awards.	AKC allows registered purebred dogs only. UKC allows mixed breed dogs to compete for titles.	• American Kennel Club (AKC) • United Kennel Club (UKC)
Conformation (Dog Show)	Dogs are judged based on how closely they resemble the standard for his breed.	For registered purebred dogs only.	• American Kennel Club (AKC) • United Kennel Club (UKC)
Freestyle	Freestyle or Dancing with Dogs is a new dog sport that uses music, a free form of heeling, and tricks.	Dogs must come when called and stay at a handler's side or heel. Dogs must know tricks and be more than six months old to compete.	• Musical Canine Sports, Inc. (MCSI) • Canine Freestyle Federation, Inc. (CFF) • World Canine Freestyle Organization Ltd. (WCFO)
Canine Good Citizen Award (CGC)	This program was design by the American Kennel Club to encourage people to help their dogs become respected members of the community.	The dog must be one year old and have a current rabies certificate. To become certified he must pass ten tests that prove he is well behaved in public places.	• American Kennel Club (AKC)
Tricks and Performance Arts	Exercise your dog's body and mind. Who knows, maybe you have the next Lassie.	Dogs must be well socialized and know how to stay in the presence of distractions. Clicker training is an asset for canine actors.	
Flyball	A fast paced relay race for your dog. Dogs jump a series of jumps, press a lever to get a ball, and then race back over the jumps.	Dogs must come when called and jump low jumps.	• North American Flyball Association, Inc. (NAFA)

Activity	Description	Requirements	Organizations
Therapy Dogs	Dogs visit and cheer up people in a variety of institutions.	Several organizations can certify well-socialized dogs for visits.	• Delta Society • Pet Therapy Dogs Incorporated • Therapy Dogs International, Inc. • Love on a Leash • Alpha Affiliates, Inc. • Therapet
Lure Coursing	Dogs chase a lure around an oval track.	Many organizations only allow specific breeds to compete. Some clubs allow all dogs to practice but only some to compete.	• NOTRA • Whippet Racing Assoc. • American Sighthound Field Association (ASFA) • Canadian Kennel Club (CKC) • Jack Russell Terrier Club of America (JRTCA)
Earthdog	Earthdog trials simulate hunting animals that live in underground dens.	These trials are limited to small terriers and dachshunds.	• The American Working Terrier Association (AWTA)
Hunting and field trials	Includes hound trials, pointing trials, and retrieving trials.		• American Kennel Club (AKC) • United Kennel Club (UKC)
Sledding, carting, weight pulling, and skijoring	These sports are great outlets for your pulling dog.	Many of these activities are open to all breeds and mixed breeds.	• Alaska Skijoring and Pulk Association • North American Skijoring and Ski Pulk Association (NASSPA)

Activity	Description	Requirements	Organizations
Herding	Dogs learn to herd sheep, ducks, and cattle with instructions from their human partner.	While many dogs herd naturally, we must teach dogs to follow our directions. Some organizations allow non-herding breeds to compete.	• Canadian Kennel Club (CKC) • Australian Shepherd Club of America (ASCA) • American Herding Breed Association (AHBA) • American Kennel Club (AKC) • United States Border Collie Handlers' Association, Inc. (USBCHA)
Tracking	Tracking can be done for fun or to find items or people.	All breeds can learn and compete in tracking.	• American Kennel Club (AKC) • National Association for Search and Rescue
Agility	Agility is a dog sport that dogs love. It is like a gigantic dog playground. Dogs run under and over obstacles while their handlers tell them which equipment to go to next.	Most agility classes require dogs to have a knowledge of basic obedience commands. They must come when called when off the leash. Dogs must be strong and healthy. They must be adults before they can compete.	• American Kennel Club (AKC) • United Kennel Club (UKC) • United States Dog Agility Association (USDAA) • Agility Association of Canada (AAC) • North American Dog Agility Council (NADAC) • Australian Shepherd Club of America (ASCA)

Stimulation

Uses

Reducing behavior problems

Reducing barking

Reducing damage

Creating fun for your dog

Dogs need mental stimulation. They often create their own stimulation if we don't find a way to satisfy their needs. Sometimes their solutions to boredom can be very distressing for us. Your dog might decide to tear up a three-hundred-dollar spa cover, as one of my student's dogs did.

If your dog is destructive while you are gone, there is nothing you can do about it after it has happened. It will do no good to punish him. You'll only hurt the relationship you have with your dog. Many dogs dig and chew when they are left alone. However, you can prevent this destructiveness with planning and teaching.

You can create a stimulating environment for your dog even when you're not at home. It can be fun. It will, however, take a little planning. Here are few suggestions to provide challenges for him.

1. Hiding food. Before leaving, distribute his meal in several hiding places. Children can help hide the food.

2. Stuffed Kongs. A Kong is a rubber dog toy that most dogs cannot chew up (see page 162). It's hollow, so you can put a variety of really great food in it. You can stuff Kongs with cheese (melt it in the Kong in the microwave), peanut butter, bread, dog cookies, or just about anything that you can think of. Just make your dog work hard to get the food out. The Kong comes with instructions.

3. Buster Cubes. This is another toy that keeps dogs busy (see page 164). You load this with treats or kibble and let your dog get it out. It also comes with instructions for use.

4. Outside toys. If your dog is an outside dog, you can rig up ropes in trees for him to tug on. Give him large indestructible toys to push around, kid's wading pools to splash in, or just about anything that gives him an outlet for his energy.

For more information on toys, see pages 162-165.

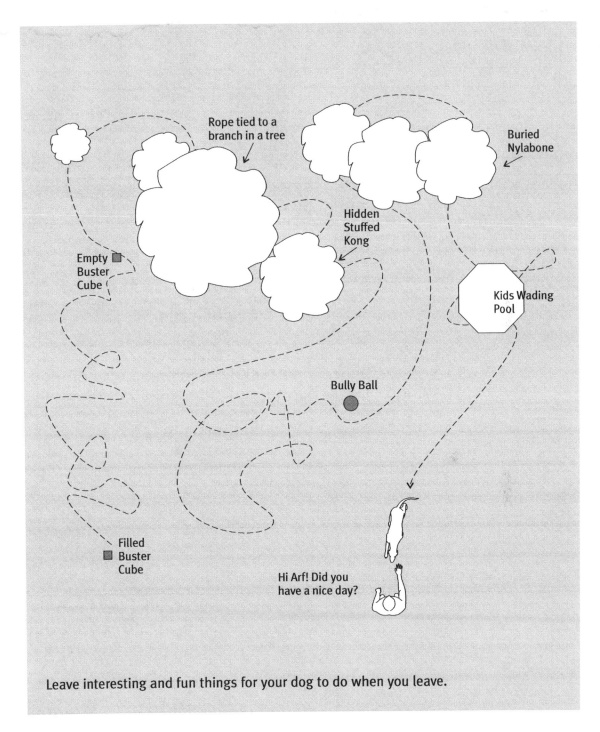

Leave interesting and fun things for your dog to do when you leave.

Peace and Quiet

Uses

Providing a quiet safe place for your dog

Aiding house training

Transporting your dog safely

All dogs need to have a place they can go to when they need to rest, or just to get away from stress. They cannot tell us when they want to left alone. We must give them access to a safe, quiet place. This could be a crate (for an appropriate time), a dog run, or a dog-proofed room. I believe dogs should live in the house, so I believe a crate is an excellent choice.

With a little clicker guidance your dog will see his crate as his own little house (see Crate Training, page 78).

Crates can serve many proposes. They are an excellent aid for house training a puppy. They provide a safe way to confine an injured dog. You can also use them to safely transport your dog.

However, crates can be used improperly. You should never put your dog in the crate for extended lengths of time. Each dog is different, but the generally accepted rule is that your puppy can stay in a crate for no more than one hour for each month of age. For example, a 4-month-old puppy should never be in it for more than four hours without being taken out for exercise, play, and potty.

There are two basic kinds of crates for pet owners, a wire one and a plastic one. Both have advantages. Many wire crates can be folded flat. However, if you ever need to ship your dog, the airlines will only allow the airline-approved plastic crates.

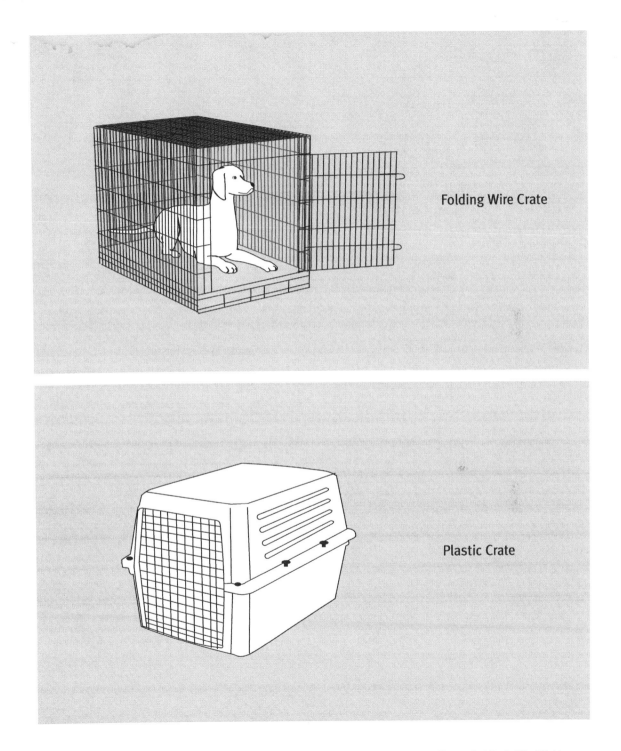

Folding Wire Crate

Plastic Crate

Understanding

Understanding your dog's body language and behavior

We have all asked our dogs to do something we think they know, like "Lie down." Instead of doing as we ask they turn their heads away from us, yawn, and slowly walk away. We get upset and decide we have a stubborn dog.

Actually, when your dog acts like this he is simply trying to communicate. He may be nervous because he doesn't understand what you expect of him. Turid Rugaas, a Norwegian dog trainer, explains in her book, *On Talking Terms With Dogs: Calming Signals*, how dogs often try to calm a situation. They can't speak to us in our language, so they use their language: body language. A yawn in dog language might mean "I am very uncomfortable with what's going on here." The dog might be frightened, or just confused and afraid of doing something wrong. Dogs are social creatures and will always try to avoid conflicts.

Another dog behavior that we often misunderstand is the learning dip (see page 184). This is a part of the normal learning process. Don't assume that your dog is stubborn because he seems to stop making progress toward your goal. Be patient. Learning dips are temporary.

The clicker is a great communication tool. It clearly signals your dog that he is doing the right thing. Clicker training helps you focus and catch him doing something right. It then gives you a way to communicate what you like. Clicker training forms a close bond between you and your dog.

Your dog is not ignoring you when he will not look at you.

Dogs don't naturally look people in the eye. They must learn that looking at our eyes is okay. Use the clicker to train your dog to look at your eyes (see page 32).

Chapter 9
Tips and Terms

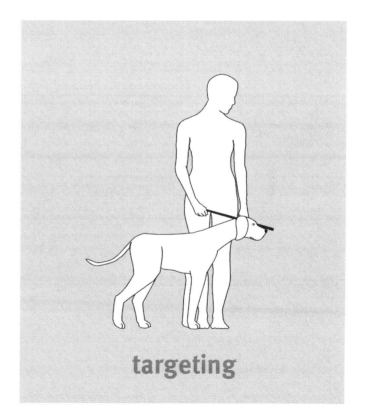

targeting

Animal Behaviorist

Applied animal behaviorists observe and treat behavior problems in animals. If your dog has serious problems, you need a qualified animal behaviorist. Your financial security and the well-being of your family could depend on your finding the right person. A qualified animal behaviorist should have an advanced degree in animal behavior or behavioral science. Ask for a detailed list of their credentials and then call the universities to verify their degrees. The person should also have experience with your type of problem.

A good animal behaviorist will give no guarantees. However, a professional behaviorist will give you a plan of action and a detailed written evaluation. They will not do a consultation over the phone or via e-mail. They will want to see your dog in his environment. Above all, they will not use any form of violence, only positive reinforcement.

Merely belonging to a professional organization does not always prove a person is qualified. Many professional organizations don't validate members' qualifications. However, the Animal Behavior Society (ABS) does certify animal behaviorists. A website for listing of certified members is at www.animalbehavior.org/Applied/directory_cert9_97.html. Another organization that can help you find an animal behaviorist is The Association of Pet Behaviour Counselors (APBC). Their e-mail address is apbc@petbcent.demon.co.uk.

Behavior Chain

A behavior chain is a series of actions or behaviors linked together like a chain by cues. You should train each part of the chain separately. The most effective way to train a chain is backwards. You train one action at a time and then link each new individual action to a previously trained action. Start with the last link in the chain and add links toward the first step in the chain. For an example of how to teach a chain see page 112.

Behavior Modification

See Operant Conditioning

Bribe

A bribe is a misuse of a reward or reinforcement. We are bribing when we must show what we are offering to get the animal (or human) to do what we want. Many people don't like to use food in dog training. They feel that they must always have food in their hands to get the dog to do as they ask. When they use food in this way they are not reinforcing good behavior, they are bribing their dog.

A bribe would be telling your child, "If you clean up your bedroom I'll take you to McDonald's." A reward or reinforcement would be if you asked her to clean her room and she did, then you took her to McDonald's as a reward for a job well done.

I believe that bribing interferes with the learning process. Your dog is so busy concentrating on the food that he's not thinking about what he is doing. To avoid bribing him, don't wave a food treat around for him to see. Put the food on a table or somewhere off your body if possible. You don't have to get the food to him immediately because the click is a promise he will get a reward. If you are teaching a skill with the magnet method (the lure method), don't keep food in your hand for more than three to five repetitions.

Collars

Martingale Style Collar

Most dogs will only need a flat collar to hold their tags on and to keep them safe on a leash. However, some dogs can slip out of a collar easily because they have large necks and small heads. A Martingale-style collar prevents this. This kind of collar tightens a limited amount so that it will not slip over your dog's head. If you need a collar like this, buy one that is adjustable. The collar should fit just tight enough not to slip over his head. The collar should rest low on his neck.

Another collar that is becoming very popular is a head halter (see Dogwise, page 194). Halter-style collars are very effective for dogs that pull. However, they can cause injury to the dog if you don't use them properly. You

Head Halter

must be very careful not to jerk your dog's head. I recommend that you have a dog trainer help you fit a head halter and show you how to use it safely.

I don't recommend using slip collars or choke chain collars. They injure many dogs. These collars are designed to 'correct' a dog. With clicker training or reinforcement training there is no reason to 'correct' your dog while training. Our goal is to reward good behavior. Choking your dog (no matter how briefly) should never be a part of training.

Crates

A crate is a portable kennel. They are available in a variety of sizes in wire or plastic.

How you introduce your dog to a crate is very important. Dogs love their crates when properly introduced to them. See page 78 to learn to teach your dog to love his crate.

Wire Crate   Plastic Crate

Cues

Cues tell your dog what he should do to get a reward. They tell your dog to start the skill or action. They are different from a command. A command tells the dog what to do to avoid being corrected. A cue tells the dog how to get a reward. Another big difference between a command and a cue is, a cue is not taught until after the dog understands how to do the skill or action.

Verbal Cue

A verbal cue can be any word, phrase, or noise. Verbal cues can be very distracting and confusing for your dog if he doesn't yet understand what he needs to do to get a click and treat. Although it sometimes seems like your dog understands your language, he really doesn't. So giving your dog a cue before he understands what he must do to get a reward would be like telling your six-year-old child, in Latin, to cook dinner.

Every dog shows you he understands how to get a click differently. Some will repeat the skill every time you pick up the clicker. Other dogs might follow you around the house showing you their new skill all day. Trainer Gary Wilkes, says "It is time to add the cue when you are willing to bet five dollars he will do the behavior."

When your dog is ready for a verbal cue, say the cue just as your dog begins the action. You want him to associate the verbal cue with what he is doing. Very gradually begin saying the cue earlier, until you are saying the cue before he begins the action.

For example, if your dog is flopping down on the ground every time you look at him, begin saying "Down" just before his elbows hit the floor. Click and toss the treat so he has to get up again to get it. Repeat saying your verbal cue just as he begins the action for several short sessions. Then begin saying "Down" before you see him beginning a down.

When he knows the meaning of a verbal cue, click and treat only when you have asked for the skill. So, if your dog runs up to you, tosses his body down, and you haven't asked him to "Down," don't reward him. Dogs don't like this part of the game. However, they soon learn the only time they can get a reward is after you give them a cue.

I have found a really fun way to add a verbal cue is to whisper it. Whispering gets your dog's attention and he focuses closely on what you are saying (remember dogs have hearing far superior to ours). Whispering your requests also works well with children.

Signal or Physical Cue

This is usually a hand signal, but it can be any nonverbal signal. It can even be an object (like an open door). When you use the magnet method (or lure your dog into position) you can turn your hand movements into a hand signal (see Magnet Method, page 26).

Add your hand signal the same way you add a verbal cue when you are not using the magnet method, or lure (see Verbal Cue, above).

Fading the Cue (or Signal)

This simply means that you make the cue smaller. Sometimes you fade it so much that only your dog can recognize it as a cue. Sometimes you replace it with another cue.

Magnet Method

To fade a cue, begin by making it only slightly smaller. Don't try to hurry this and reduce the signal too fast. Fading the cue too fast will only make it harder for your dog to understand what you want. An example of fading the cue can be found on page 106.

To Change the Cue (or signal)

To change one cue to another, for example a verbal cue to a hand signal, first give the hand signal (the new cue). Next give the verbal cue (the old cue). Giving the new cue first is important. Put a great deal of emphasis on it. Once your dog begins to respond to the new cue, gradually begin dropping the old one.

Hand Signal　See Cues/Signal or Physical Cue

Jackpot　We all love good surprises. Dogs are the same. A jackpot is a surprise of an extra big reward. It is something good and unexpected. In clicker training we often surprise the dog by giving him a 'jackpot' of extra treats. When my dog has a 'breakthrough' or a big jump in learning, I give him the treat he earned and then also play with him as an extra reward.

Latent Learning　Latent learning is when a dog appears to learn between teaching sessions. Many clicker trainers have observed that their dog's skills improve between sessions. I have also experienced this and am always amazed. My dog not only remembers what he has learned between sessions, but sometimes his new skill improves (even when the sessions are months apart).

Learning Dip (also known as a Pre-Learning Dip)　Learning does not progress evenly. Every person and every animal learns at his own rate. A normal part of the learning process is a learning dip. Your dog will be progressing toward a goal and then suddenly seem to forget what he has already learned. The dogs may walk off or just quit. This is only temporary. Often he will return on his own and begin making very fast progress.

Why do dogs do this? It doesn't really matter. What is important is to understand that this is normal and temporary. Do not be discouraged. Let him return and start again the next time he is interested in earning a click.

Operant and Classical Conditioning

These are scientific terms used to explain how animals (including humans) learn. Clicker training is based on the principles of Operant Conditioning.

Operant Conditioning

B. F. Skinner coined this term. With operant conditioning the animal uses his actions to control his environment. He rings the bell to get the door to open. He learns that his action makes the door open.

Classical, Respondent, or Pavlovian Conditioning

With Classical Conditioning the animal responds to his environment without conscious actions. His action does not affect the consequences. The dog hears the bell ring. The ringing bell tells him the door will open. He is conditioned to expect the door to open when he hears the door bell ring.

Qualified Clicker Instructors

Currently no organizations in the United States are licensing dog training instructors. Anyone can take out an ad in the yellow pages and call himself an expert. The only way that you can be sure to find the best instructor for you and your dog is to interview them and ask hard questions. To find a list of possible clicker instructors near you, check the website www.wazoo.com/~marge/Clicker_Trainers/Clicker_Trainers. html. Before you sign up for a class use the forms on pages 134-137. Then decide if the trainers are following the principles of clicker training.

Clicker training is becoming very popular. Many instructors feel all they need to do is use a clicker occasionally and they can claim they are clicker trainers. This is not fair to you and your dog. Clicker training is scientific training that is founded in established principles.

Ask prospective instructors about their formal training or education (including seminars). Very few instructors have extensive training and experience in clicker training. Marine animal trainers are an exception. They have been using the principles of clicker training for many years. Some marine animal trainers have now become dog clicker instructors.

Many good instructors use the same scientific principles used by clicker trainers. However, they do not use a clicker. It is important to find an instructor who understands and can apply these scientific training principles. When looking for an instructor, remember they will not be training your dog — they will be training you. You must find someone that can explain what you need to do, so you can understand and teach it to your dog. Some instructors are excellent dog trainers. They can train dogs to do wonderful things, but cannot tell you how to teach your dog.

The best way to learn more is to educate yourself. Read books about clicker training, join computer e-mail clicker lists, read Internet sites, attend seminars, and watch videos (see pages 192-195).

Release Word

This is a word that tells your dog when he is finished. It ends the game or skill. You can use any word(s) that you want. I like the word "Release." I don't recommend that you use "Okay." People use this word often in everyday conversation and it can confuse a dog. A recent personal event taught me why using "Okay" can be dangerous. My dog was in the backseat of my car. I needed to open the back door on the traffic side to unbuckle him from his seatbelt. A passenger in my car asked me a question. I answered "Okay" as I undid my dog's buckle. He jumped out into oncoming traffic. He came when I called, and avoided being hit. He got a big treat for coming. I then retrained him to wait in the car until he hears the release word "Out."

Shaping

Shaping is a proven method for increasing the likelihood of a desired action being repeated. We use several shaping methods in clicker training.

Pure Shaping, also known as Free shaping, or Successive Approximation

Without luring or prompting the action, reward each small increment (baby steps) that will eventually add up to the complete skill or game. See page 188 for a game to help you understand how to teach your dog this way.

Magnet Method or Luring

Move your dog by leading him around with food in your hand. While this method gets the action started, it does have drawbacks. See information about bribing on page 181. A more effective form of luring is target training (see page 96).

Capturing (also known as lazy trainer method or couch training)
This is the easiest method to use. You simply wait until your dog does what you want and then click at the exact moment he does it. Then follow with a reward. An example of this type of training is given on page 28.

Going Back to Kindergarten
I first heard Karen Pryor use this term at a *Don't Shoot the Dog* seminar. She explained that if your dog seems to have a problem learning, you must go back in your training process as far as necessary for him to be successful. If your dog is not frequently earning clicks, go back to the step where you were clicking frequently. Then slowly begin adding small steps toward your goal.

Signal

See Cues

Starting Signal

See Cues

Systematic Desensitization

This is a method used by psychologists and behaviorists to help get a person or animal over a fear. Dog trainers use it often to help dogs get used to a variety of places, objects, and events that upsetting them. Clicker training can speed up desensitization tremendously.

Click and treat your dog for every small action he takes in overcoming his fear. Don't force him. Let your dog decide when he wants to move closer to what is frightening to him. An example of systematic desensitization is crate training (see page 78).

If your dog fears people, you may need to consult a qualified animal behaviorist to help you develop a desensitization plan (see page 180).

Targeting

Many zoo and marine animal trainers control the movements of animals with targeting. A target can be anything, a stick, a hand, a Post-It note, etc. You click and treat your dog for touching the object. Then you move the object around and click and treat him for following the object (see pages 96-99).

Training Game

This is a fun game to play with people. It helps you learn how clicker training works (See the game rules on page 189). You play this game like the children's Hot and Cold game. With the training game the trainer directs the person playing the animal with clicks and treats toward the selected goal.

Teach this game to your kids. They'll love it.

Verbal Cue

See Cues

Verbal Marker

A verbal marker is a word that replaces the click. Clicker trainers use the verbal marker the same way they use the clicker. It marks the exact second that your dog does the correct action. The verbal marker is not as accurate as the clicker, and therefore you should only use it after your dog learns the skill. Clicker trainers begin using a verbal marker when they wish to start fading out the clicker. An example of a verbal marker would telling the dog "YESSSS" or "Excellent" instead of clicking. See Fading the Clicker (page 124).

The Training Game	
Equipment:	Clicker People treats (chocolate kisses are great)
Players:	Two. One person plays the trainer and one person plays the animal. Audience. (Optional)
Instructions for playing the game:	1. Send the animal/person out of the room. 2. The audience or trainer selects a specific action for the animal/person to do. This action can be anything physically possible and not embarrassing to the animal/person. Some suggestions might be to turn off the light switch, touch the wall, or sit in a specific chair. Be creative. 3. The trainer invites the animal/person back into the room. 4. The trainer asks the animal/person to begin moving about the room. 5. The trainer clicks the animal/person for getting close to the chosen goal action. 6. The animal/person must stop what she is doing and go back to the trainer to get a treat when she hears a click. 7. The trainer continues to click actions that get closer to the chosen goal until the animal/person does the goal action. 8. After the animal/person successfully completes the game, players choose a new animal/person and a new trainer so everyone has a chance to experience both sides. *Note:* Remember, the trainer (or audience) cannot give any signals or verbal cues to the animal/person.

Chapter 10
Resources

Clicker Training Web Sites

www.clickertraining.com; also **www.clickerpet.com**

Karen Pryor's home page. Information on clicker training a wide range of animals (including humans) from the person who started clicker training. Supplies and books, articles, news, clicker honor roll.

www.click-l.com

Kathleen Weaver's excellent training site. Includes links to supplies, listservs.

www.geocities.com/Athens/Academy/8636/Clicker.html

This site has an excellent explanation of operant conditioning by Stacy Braslau-Schneck, M.A. The site also contains a list of links to other clicker web sites (even non-English sites).

www.geocities.com/Heartland/Meadows/4159/pawsplus.html

Elizabeth TeSelle's site, with information about clicker training.

www.shirleychong.com/keepers/

Six lessons by Shirley Chong, originally published as a challenge for trainers on her clicker e-mail list. Also a list of articles voted as 'keepers' by the members of clicker e-mail lists.

www.wazoo.com/~marge/Clicker_Trainers/Clicker_Trainers.html

Marge Morgan's List of clicker trainers. This is a list of people who have chosen to be added to this list. It is a good start to look for a local clicker trainer, however, there is no guarantee of their knowledge of clicker training.

www.clickandtreat.com

Gary Wilke's home page. Information and supplies for clicker training.

Other Dog-Related Web Sites

www.dog-play.com/

One of my favorite sites for information on dogs and dog activities, with a huge number of links to organizations and other web sites.

www.traveldog.com

Site for information about traveling with your dog.

Books

Clicker Training for Obedience, by Morgan Spector, 1999, Sunshine Books.

The Culture Clash, by Jean Donaldson, 1996, James & Kenneth Publishers. Not a how-to book, but it helps understand dogs and how to train them.

The Dog Whisperer, by Paul Owens, 1999, Adams Media Corp.

Getting Started: Clicker Training for Dogs, kit by Karen Pryor, 1999, Sunshine Books. This book includes "A Dog and a Dolphin," a clicker training classic; Easy instructions; Frequently Asked Questions; and Resources. Sold in a kit: the book, two clickers, treats.

The Perfect Puppy, by Gwen Bailey, 1995, Reader's Digest Books. This book does not tell you how to use a clicker, but it's the best puppy book I have found. You can apply the clicker to any of the behaviors in this book. Also, useful information for adult dog owners.

On Talking Terms with Dogs: Calming Signals, by Turid Rugaas, 1997, Legacy-by-Mail. This is not a book on how to clicker train, it is a small book on how to understanding your dog's behavior.

The Toolbox for Remodeling Problem Behaviors, by Terry Ryan, 1998, Howell Book House. A very good general dog book. Not only for curing problems, but for preventing them.

Operant Conditioning Books

Don't Shoot the Dog! The New Art of Teaching and Training, revised edition, by Karen Pryor, 1999, Bantam Doubleday Dell. This is the book that started it all. Not about dogs, it's about training all animals and people without punishment. The book does a terrific job of explaining practical applications of operant conditioning to everyday life. The revised edition contains a chapter on clicker training. www.clickerpet.com.

Lads Before the Wind: Diary of a Dolphin Trainer, expanded edition, by Karen Pryor, 2000, Sunshine Books. www.clickerpet.com

Books (continued)

On Behavior, by Karen Pryor, 1995, Sunshine Books.

About Behaviorism, by B. F. Skinner, 1976, Vintage Books.

Science and Human Behavior, by B. F. Skinner, 1965, The Free Press.

Videos

Clicker Magic: The Art of Clicker Training, by Karen Pryor. This video combines theory with actual multi-species training sessions. It even shows clicker training a fish. www.clickerpet.com.

Puppy Love: Raise Your Dog the Clicker Way, by Karen Pryor. The all-positive way to fit a puppy or new dog into your home without strife. www.clickerpet.com.

Take a Bow Wow I and II. This is an excellent how-to video for training practical tricks with the clicker. It's good for all ages. (Caution! In this video they occasionally click without giving a treat. Research has shown that this will lessen the power of the clicker.) www.dogwise.com.

Click & Treat Training Kit, by Gary Wilkes. www.click&treat.com.

Clicker Training Supplies

www.karenpryor.com and Sunshine Books, Inc. Publisher and distributor of books, videos, clickers, and target sticks for positive reinforcement and clicker training.
> 800-47CLICK or 781-398-0754
> www.clickertraining.com; www.karenpryor.com;
> www.clickerpet.com

Dogwise Book Catalog from Direct Books. Books, clickers, bait bags, head halters, toys, and videos
> 800-776-2665; www.dogwise.com

Legacy-by-Mail. Books, videos, and training supplies.
> 888-876-9364; www.legacy-by-mail.com.

Dog-Related Associations

Agility Association of Canada (AAC)
RR#2
Lucan, ON, Canada N0N 2J0
519 657-7636
www.aac.ca

Alaska Skijoring and Pulk Association
P.O. Box 82843
Fairbanks, AK, USA 99708-2843

Alpha Affiliates, Inc.
PO Box 176
Mendham, NJ, USA 07945-0176
973 539-2770
Fax 973 644-0610
e-mail: AlphaAffiliates@webtv.net
www.caninetimes.com/NonProfits/alphaafilli-
ate/index.htm

American Border Collie Association
82 Rogers Road
Perkinston, MS, USA 39573-8843
601 928-7551 (voice)
601 928-5148 (fax)
e-mail:ABCA@datasync.com
www.bordercollie.org/abca.html

American Herding Breed Association
(AHBA)
Allows all breeds
Lisa Allen, Membership Coordinator
277 Central Ave.
Seekonk, MA, USA 02771
508 761-4078
e-mail: pecans@ix.netcom.com
www.primenet.com/~joell/ahba/main.htm

American Kennel Club (AKC)
51 Madison Ave.
New York, NY, USA 10010
212 696-8200
Fax 212 696-8299
www.americankennelclub.com/index.html

American Sighthound Field Association (ASFA)
Susan Weinkein, President
923 Shagbark Drive
Nevada, IA , USA 50201
Home 515 382-3047
Work 515 239-2415
Fax 515 239-5092
e-mail: Weinkein@aol.com
www.asfa.org/

The American Working Terrier Association
(AWTA)
e-mail gitemgang@yahoo.com
www.dirt-dog.com/awta/index.shtml

Association of Pet Behaviour Counsellors
P.O. Box 46
Worcester, England WR89YS
44-1386-751151
e-mail apbc@petbcent.demon.co.uk
www.apbc.org.uk/

Australian Shepherd Club of America
(ASCA)
6091 East State Highway 21
Bryan, TX, USA 77803-9652
409 778-1082
e-mail: asca@mail.myriad.net
www.asca.org

The British Flyball Association
PO Box 263
Fareham, Hants PO16 0XB
+44 1730 828269
Fax +44 1726 861079
www.flyball.org.uk/

Canadian Kennel Club (CKC)
89 Skyway Avenue, Suite 100
Etobicoke, ON, Canada M9W 6R4
800 250-8040 or 416 675-5511
Fax 416 675-6506
e-mail: information@ckc.ca
www.ckc.ca/

Canine Freestyle Federation, Inc.
Monica Patty
21900 Foxden Lane
Leesburg, VA, USA 20175
www.canine-freestyle.org/

Delta Society Pet Partners Programs
289 Perimeter Rd. East
Renton, WA., USA 98055
800 869-6898
Fax 206 235-1076
e-mail: info@deltasociety.org
www.deltasociety.org

Jack Russell Terrier Club of America
(JRTCA)
P.O. Box 4527
Lutherville, MD, USA 21094-4527
410 561-3655
Fax 410 560-2563
JRTCA@worldnet.att.net
www.terrier.com/

The United Kingdom Kennel Club
1-5 Clarges Street
London, England W1Y8AB
www.The-kennel-club.org.uk/

Musical Canine Sports International, Inc.
Sharon Tutt, Treasurer/Membership Chair
16665 Parkview Place
Surrey, BC, Canada V4N 1Y8
604 581-3641

National Association for Search and Rescue
4500 Southgate Pl.,Stuite 100
Chantilly, VA, USA 22021
703 222-6277
www.nasar.org

North American Dog Agility Council
(NADAC)
HCR 2, Box 277
St. Maries, ID, USA 83861
208 689-3803
e-mail NADACKA@aol.com
www.nadac.com

North American Flyball Association, Inc.
1400 W. Devon Ave, #512
Chicago, IL, USA 60660.
www.flyball.org/index.html

North American Skijoring and Ski Pulk
Association(NASSPA)
P.O. Box 240573
Anchorage, AK, USA 99524
907 349-WOOF
www.ptialaska.net/~skijor/

Therapet
P.O. Box 1696
Shari Bernard OTR
Whitehouse, TX, USA 75791-1696
email: Therapet@Juno.com

Therapy Dogs International, Inc.
88 Bartley Road
Flanders, NJ, USA 07836
973 252-9800
973 252-7171 (fax)
e-mail: Therapy Dogs International
tdi@gti.net

Therapy Dogs Incorporated
P.O. Box 5868
Cheyenne, WY, USA 82003
877 843-7364
e-mail: therdaog@gisna.com

United Kennel Club (UKC)
100 E. Kilgore Road
Kalamazoo, MI, USA 49001-5593
616 343-9020
www.ukcdogs.com

United States Border Collie Handlers'
Association, Inc. (USBCHA)
2915 Anderson Lane
Crawford, TX, USA 76638
254 486-2500
Fax 254 486-2271
e-mail f.raley@worldnet.att.net
www.bordercollie.org/club.html

United States Dog Agility Association
(USDAA)
P.O. Box 850995
Richardson, TX, USA 75085-0955
972 231-9700
e-mail info@usdaa.com
www.usdaa.com

World Canine Freestyle Organization Ltd.
P.O. Box 350122
Brooklyn, NY, USA 11235-2525
718 332-5238
Fax 718 646-2686
e-mail: wcfodogs@aol.com
www.woofs.org/wcfo

Acknowledgments

**I have stood
on the shoulders
of giants...**

– Isaac Newton

The information in this book has been inspired by clicker trainers around the world. They have shared suggestions and solutions for finding kinder and gentler ways to train our canine friends. I have learned from many of these wonderful creative and supportive people both in person and on computer email lists like Click-l, Clicktrain, and ClickTeach.

A special thanks to my students and their dogs. My students asked the hard questions and their dogs taught all of us what works best. People like Kathy Sdao, Maggie Tia Tucker, the Babbs, Carol Boyd, and Barry Tillman helped me find the answers, encouraged me, and helped put those answers in this book.

And of course thanks to Karen Pryor for introducing me to clicker training and for being a wonderful editor who inspired me to do my best.

About the Author

Peggy Larson Tillman, with her husband Barry Tillman, is a pioneer in the science of ergonomics: designing machines and environments so that they fit, physically and behaviorally, with human beings. They have authored two leading texts in the field, handbooks liberally laced with Peggy Tillman's computer drawings. Peggy's drawings—behaviorally sensitive, often truly beautiful, and always highly informative—are the heart of this book.

Peggy Tillman also worked for many years as an elementary school teacher. She discovered clicker training when she acquired her standard poodle, Charles. Clicker work fit exactly with her concept of how children should be treated: fairly, and with lots of opportunities to succeed. Charles endorsed the clicker approach. Peggy went on to teach classes to many, many pet owners, and in the process evolved her own visual instructional material. This book is the happy result.

The Tillmans and Charles live on an island in Puget Sound, near Seattle. Peggy Tillman may be reached at www.magicpaws.com or hfengineering@prodigy.net.

Index

T